RELIGION AND THE WESTERN MIND

Religion and the Western Mind

Ninian Smart
Professor of Religious Studies
University of California, Santa Barbara

State University of New York Press

First published
in USA by
STATE UNIVERSITY OF NEW YORK PRESS
Albany

For information, address State University of New York
Press, State University Plaza, Albany, NY 12246

Printed in Hong Kong

Library of Congress Cataloging-in-Publication Data
Smart, Ninian, 1927–
Religion and the western mind.
Portions delivered as the Drummond Lectures,
University of Stirling, March 1985.
Bibliography: p.
Includes index.
1. Religion—Study and teaching.   2. Religions—
Study and teaching.   I. Title.
BL41.S596   1986   200'.7   86–10578
ISBN 0–88706–382–9
ISBN 0–88706–383–7 (pbk.)

In memory of Eddie

Contents

Contents

Preface

The heart of this book is the Drummond Lectures delivered at the University of Stirling in March 1985. To an expanded version of the three lectures I have added a number of papers, both published and unpublished, on topics related to the themes explored in the lectures.

The Drummonds, in Part I 'Religion and the Western Mind', present the exciting and explosive possibilities of the modern study of religion. Religions and, more generally, worldviews, have the power to help shape history, but are often left out of account with the modern preoccupation with economic and political forces. The modern study of religion attempts to delineate and explain the nature and effects of worldviews, and is in principle plural in its coverage of world religions. The lectures contain an indictment of the establishmentarian stance of much Christian theology and the analogous missionary stance of much philosophy, and contains criticisms of the way the lines are drawn in much of education. It is also important for the reader to enter into some of the crucial contributions of Religious Studies to contemporary intellectual life.

Chapter 4, 'Christianity and Nationalism' propounds a theory about nations' need for ideological and religious justifications of the sacrifices they demand, and considers what a Christian should say to this, standing, so to speak as a citizen of heaven, in a position to criticize. In Chapter 5, 'Resurgence and Identity in Three Faiths' I examine three movements – the Moral Majority, the Muslim Brotherhood and the Gush Emunim in Israel – similar backlashes not necessarily auguring well for the libertarian position argued in this book. Chapter 6, 'The Dynamics of Religion and Political Change' looks at the contrasting situations of Sri Lanka and India in trying to cope with Western influence and intrusion during both the colonial period and its aftermath, and delineates the Indian tradition in a new way. Chapter 7, 'The Future of Religions' employs some of the methods outlined in the rest of the book in trying to diagnose the future. The final chapter 'A Global Ethic' explores the ethical inferences that can be drawn from the epistemology of worldviews, and supports a position which runs like a thread through the book, namely soft non-relativism. The conclusions are in my view invigorating.

I was greatly honoured by the invitation to give the Drummond Lectures, especially because my father was born and raised a few miles from Stirling's wonderful campus, in Doune, and so the area is dear to me. I was shown great hospitality and kindness by Glyn and Helga Richards during our stay in Scotland and by the Principal and Lady Alexander. I also wish to remember Eddie Stamp, a famous accounting theorist and a good friend, for coming up from Lancaster to listen – an incarnation of that wider audience that I would like my thoughts in this volume to reach. I believe that the modern study of religion should occur in the context of a radical reappraisal of our education system in the West.

Lancaster   NINIAN SMART

Acknowledgements

The article 'Christianity and Nationalism' appeared in *The Scottish Journal of Religious Studies*, vol. v, no. 1 (spring, 1984); 'The Dynamics of Religious and Political Change: Illustrations from South Asia' in *Bangalore Theological Forum*, vol. xvi (May–August 1984), and 'The Future of Religions' in *Futures* (February 1985). We acknowledge, with thanks, permission to reproduce these essays here.

I
Religion and the Western Mind

1

Religious Studies and
the Western Mind

One of the great achievements of modern scholarship is the invention of the modern study of religion.[1] It ought to be an essential element of education. It is illuminating and disturbing, and its coming has often hardly been noticed in the rest of academia. Its messages often do not penetrate the conceptual wall which images of religion put up around the rationalist mind, and it is often clouded by the fog generated by older theological models of the study of religion. But the plural, crosscultural, multi-disciplinary exploration of religion and, more generally, of the worldviews which help to shape human action has some powerful thoughts to suggest to the rest of the social sciences and humanities.

One of the most powerful of these is the thought that our Western attitudes are still often colonialist and tribal. We have not absorbed the lessons of the World Parliament of Religions of 1893, in which Vivekananda eloquently projected a new voice from the East. We often think of history, world history, in terms of a line from Abraham to Reagan, and of literature as a Western phenomenon, and of anthropology as applicable to them and not to us, and of psychoanalytic accounts of religion as verified by an account of late 19th Century Victorian religion, and of philosophy as Western philosophy, and of society as typically Western society, and of morality as our morality, or of our morality as morality. It is true that matters have improved in this respect since World War II, but we still have not grasped the double revolution of *epoche*, of crosscultural bracketing.

For it is such bracketing that lies, methodologically, at the heart of the modern study of religion. The jargon is drawn from Husserl, but the practice and the message differ from his. The practice, which is somewhat dialectical, involves trying to present the beliefs, symbols and activities of the other (and who that is I shall

3

come to in a moment) from the perspective of that other. The presuppositions, feelings and attitudes of the explorer of the other's world must be bracketed out as far as possible. That is, we should not bring external judgments to bear upon the other's world. The practice of such bracketing is, as I have said, somewhat dialectical, and the reason for this is that we have to make his or her 'other' worldview and meanings available to the consciousness and culture of ourselves.

Why should we not bring external, namely our, judgments to bear on the other's world? If it is Hitler's values we are exploring, surely we *need* to bring judgment to bear. Here, however, even with Hitler the Native American proverb applies: 'Never judge a person till you have walked a mile in his moccasins.' If you genuinely entered in to the Nazi worldview, incidentally, you might come out more, not less, frightened: part of the problem was that often Western leaders did not bother to understand, or, worse, superficially sympathized with Hitler's aims. The reason why we should enter in to someone else's worldview is not, however, sentimental. It is not, conversely, a matter of being coldly neutral. It is not a matter of losing feelings: for empathy means 'feeling in' the other: entering imaginatively into the other's feelings, as well as her beliefs and so on. The reason it is important is that we want to get at the facts. What Hitler thought and felt and did were facts. The inner facts about Hitler help to explain a lot of the outer ones, and we need to know the inner Hitler as well as we can, if we wish to understand the terrible history of those times. Likewise if we wish to explore the nature of Buddhism we need to get at the meanings which are held by the Buddhist texts and Buddhist people. *Our* views are not facts about *them*, but facts about us. Later, when we have found out what Buddhist Buddhism is we can shape our own. Naturally, there are some hermeneutic questions about how far this ideal of bracketing out our own presuppositions is possible, but I shall assume for the time being that there is the possibility of genuine bracketing, and that it involves a meaningful migration into the mind of the other.

The study of religion is not alone in demanding such a stance. It is intrinsic to much in anthropology, sociology and other disciplines. But it has been stressed most strongly in the study of religion. It is of course not the whole of religious method, but it is an essential ingredient, this informed or structured empathy whereby we travel into the minds of other people. It has wide educational implications which we often neglect. In fact the education system undervalues the virtues and noble advantages of empathy. Let me pause to celebrate this glory of empathy.

To see the world through another person's eyes: is this not a noble task? For a boy to know something of what it is like to be a girl, for a lover to see herself through the eyes of *her* lover, to see the problems of one's mother-in-law, to imagine what it is like to be a starving Ethiopian or a Tamil, to conceive the thought world of the ordinary Russian or Romanian or Italian – all these are fine exercises of the human imagination, and very practical too. But how much effort is put into these mental and emotional migrations by our educational systems? Literature and drama do it somewhat, which is why both should be encouraged as part of the crosscultural study of religion. But very often politically we are pressed to reaffirm *our* values, *our* history, *our* religion (whatever that is), *our* worldview; and politically it is sometimes very hard to achieve migrations into the worlds of the other.

But who is the other? This is in effect the same question as the definition of *crosscultural*, which I have used as one of the defining characteristics of the modern study of religion. To say that the study of religion is crosscultural is to say that it often and typically involves people in Culture A studying people and ideas in Culture B. At a gross or macrosociological level, a culture is a whole society or group of societies, such as Europe or North America or even both, considered as the entity 'Western culture'. The study of religion thus typically involves work which crosses the cultural frontiers, into the East and the South. But also even within a society there are other traditions: increasingly so, with the migration of so many people across national frontiers – so that Los Angeles and Birmingham, England, are multicultural cities. There are Jews living beside Christians, and Muslims living beside Sikhs and Confucianists – and so forth. So 'crosscultural' also means 'across traditions'. But in describing some group as Christian or Jewish or Buddhist we are still very much at a macrosociological level. The Catholic differs from the Baptist and the Copt, and the Iranian Shi'i from the Arabian Wahhabi or the Indonesian Sunni. Every major tradition collapses into a shoal of subtraditions, and this is without even counting the new traditions and religions that form along the boundaries between

traditions and cultures. And even within Methodism or Con-
gregationalism there are of course varieties of faith and practice.
The fact, incidentally, that two subtraditions or sub-subtraditions
are historically close does not mean that they are emotionally
close. It may be harder to empathize with your neighbour than
with the cousin or stranger.

Despite these qualifications, the macrosociological meanings of
'crosscultural' are not to be neglected, for they symbolize something important for our world – that the study of religion is
essentially plural, crossing boundaries of the human mind, and
extending if possible indeed to the whole globe: both across
national boundaries and across traditional boundaries betwen
religions and worldviews. In being crosscultural like this, the
modern study of religion is the antithesis of the standpoint of the
older, theological model.

For it is only on some sufferance that Buddhism, or even Roman
Catholicism, can enter into the Faculty of Divinity in one of our
ancient Scottish universities. It is true that theology has, to its
credit, an open and critical attitude to the Christian scriptures:
but in the last resort traditional theology was in the business of
training the clergy – and not any clergy, but specifically the
ministers of the Kirk in Scotland, Anglican clergy in Oxbridge
and Roman clerics in Rome. In the last resort therefore theology
was committed to a particular standpoint, a special worldview. It
did not need to pretend to be openminded. Naturally, things
within the theological ambit have changed a lot since World War
II especially: but in principle the tradition has not in the past
been plural in emphasis, nor now is it very plural. Ecumenism,
by homogenizing Christians, has not increased greatly pluralism:
it has, however, made relations between Christian organizations
greatly more civil and friendly, except of course for those who
reject ecumenism. To some of these issues I shall return: for the
general lack of pluralism of traditional theology is reflected in
part of the educational scene, in so far as many folk see religious
education as essentially Christian in this country. But, as I say,
the modern study of religion is consciously, almost aggressively,
crosscultural and plural. And it is an essential ingredient in education in so far as this world which we live in is plural.

I have, however, often been met by an observation in this
regard. When Donald Horder and I and other colleagues were
working with teachers in the troubled province of Northern

Ireland, in the early 1970s, we were sometimes upbraided for mentioning Buddhism. An interviewer once asked me on Irish TV: 'Surely you do not mean that you would teach Buddhism to children in Northern Ireland?' He said it in a professionally scandalized tone of voice. 'Some accent on non-violence', I replied, 'would do no harm.' But my answer was, of course, a little bit disingenuous. We were teaching about Buddhism to affirm the principle of pluralism, and to try to show how a religion could be taught coolly and without prejudice.[2] Yet sometimes our friends in Belfast or Coleraine did complain that some of this material was remote from the world of Northern Ireland. Their assumption seemed to be that their children would never move, that Buddhism and Hinduism would never be found in the Province as they are to be found in Birmingham, Los Angeles and Paris, that their world would, in effect, not change, and that anything extraneous could be shut out. Already, though, TV was showing these wider worlds. In short, our children are entering into a new global civilization: the standards of the 1950s are not good enough to cope with their future. I would consider cultural tribalism always to be wrong: but it is especially egregious when we now live in a global civilization.

The price of ostrich feathers in South Africa depends on the whims of *Vogue*; of gold in New York on the stability of the dollar, itself an index of worldwide currency fluctuations; of copper in Zambia on the degree to which Californian electricians move into plastic; of wheat in Arkansas on the winter in Soviet Central Asia; of cloth in Delhi on the market in Hong Kong; of tea in Sri Lanka on the auctions in London. Satellites meanwhile beam world varieties of television into homes in Madras and Bangkok and Wigan. Jets ply ceaselessly between world capitals. Germans buy villas in Tenerife, Scandinavians in Senegal, French in the Seychelles, and tides of tourism are engulfing even the remotest areas such as Papua New Guinea. Islands across the Pacific are threatened with bikinis. And behind it all about 500 multinational companies rule the world, conjointly with some of the larger national governments, anonymously out of Nassau, Tokyo and California, and wherever the chief executives of multinationals choose to gather. It is a new imperialism, but without an imperial country. We are being bound together by shipments, telephone calls, aeroplanes, tankers, freight exchanges and electronic pulses. The globe is achieving economic unity, and the older model of the nation-State as being the community of ultimate concern is withering before new economic forces and new conceptualizations of human living. We are moving decisively into the transnational epoch and the age of the globe. It is therefore madness to neglect the human beliefs and values of the great religions, for they have their distinctive motifs to add to this global civilization.

At this point a different kind of objection may be heard. There are those who think that religion is on the way out. It is obsolescent: a bundle or a series of bundles of wishfulfilling absurdities, an amalgam of old cosmologies now superseded by scientific thinking, a mass of symbols without rational basis, illusions departing slowly from the scene as rational education and technological advances make their impact on human lives. There are therefore those who, far from thinking that education in religion is an essential ingredient in education, would like to wish it away. They think of it as pernicious and darkening. It is not the business of education to spread obscurantism, they think.

To such an objection there is a two-fold reply: one to do with power and empathy: the other to do with the definition of our field. As to the first: the power of Islam in Iran, Libya or Indonesia is *there*, independently of what we (whoever we are) think of the rationality or otherwise of the beliefs held by the leaders and activists of these societies. Buddhism in Sri Lanka has its influence independently of our judgment about it. Christianities retain a degree of power and vitality: the measurement of these is a major task of the sociologist of religion. So knowing about these matters is positively important in the new global civilization. Moreover, the modern study of religion, in so far as it tries to be phenomenological, tries to present these faiths without either endorsing or rejecting them. Whatever beauties and defects they may have in the eyes of the beholder it is not because of our teaching these religions as if they were *true* or *false*.

But in addition, from what viewpoint is religion seen to be on the way out? And what counts as religion? Here it is important to stand back and look at the very category 'religious'. It is open to question from various points of view. First, there is much controversy as to whether there is any ultimately satisfactory definition of the term. There have been some powerful modern critiques of the Western conception of religion – notably in W. C. Smith's *The Meaning and End of Religion*. Not only this, but we cannot fail to reflect that if the modern study of religion (or rather its analogue) had developed in India or China in the first place we might have had the comparative study of *dharma* or the cros-scultural investigation of different *Taos*. And would that not have included Marxisms as well as Christianities? So we need at least to be sceptical about hard-lined definitions of religion.

But more important than this observation is the thought of continuities both in life and education. Scientific humanism and Marxism are often in living contact and conflict with traditionally religious belief-systems. Rivals should be treated together. If they are not, then we are taking steps to entrench some determinate viewpoint into our educational system, and genuine pluralism is in this way eroded. Sometimes indeed we have arrived at the regrettable state of affairs in which a philosophy department may regard itself as teaching rationality and scientific humanism in ideological contrast to the crypto-religious teaching purveyed by a religion department. It is a regrettable state of affairs because it entrenches selection of personnel by reference to the accept-ibility of their beliefs; but it is regrettable also because it is not an honest situation. If the institution of religion or of philosophy means the imposition upon the university of a worldview not derived essentially from the nature of the university we are back with at least a mild case of discrimination against outsiders.

But at a deeper level, the false division between religion and philosophy (or rather an aspect of philosophy) is bad, though normal because it reflects one of a number of absurdities in the way in which we carve up the academic world. A student who wishes to study Sartre probably has to go to French Studies; Mao, and it is Chinese Studies; Vivekananda or Tillich, to Religious Studies; Wittgenstein, Kant or Chomsky, to Philosophy; Marx, to Political Science; the worldview of the Masai, to Anthropology; and Theodore Herzl, to Jewish Studies. Yet all those people and ideas are expressing worldviews – overlapping, sometimes in conflict, often presenting themselves for choice. It does not make sense that academic studies are in this respect so fragmented. To some extent, the trouble is that we have evolved differing canoni-cal traditions: we have defined the past in terms of modern philosophy, for instance, and so define a canonical line as genuine philosophers. Often some thinkers may be banished: for a long time in Anglo-Saxon philosophy (predominantly ordinary-lan-guage and analytic) it was not possible to discuss Heidegger or

Sartre: and to a great degree Indian and Chinese philosophy are also outcaste. The irrational division of the study of worldviews among the various departmental disciplines is reinforced in modern times by the globalization of academia. David Lodge's *Small World* is no joke: now international seminars, congresses, publications, correspondences tend to run along formalized lines, and the lines tend to be those already set by the state of academia in the 1960s and 1970s. Canons now can become transnational, and their validity is given a spurious global recognition.

Part of the problem of the fragmentation of the treatment of worldviews stems from the distinction between fact and value, between analysis and evaluation. Philosophy is explicitly in the business of making judgments: it is history of philosophy which is concerned with the description and analysis of the ideas as they have come to be excogitated in human life. Now since history of philosophy is history of *philosophy* it is natural that much attention be paid to those people and events which relate to issues currently debated by philosophers, and so there is a trend to select as philosophers those who count as such from this current perspective. Similarly in literature there is the tendency to create a canon from those counted now for whatever reasons as 'good' authors. On the other hand in Chinese studies there is less concern with whether Mao is good or not or even whether his worldview or parts of it will long survive. More vital has been the actual power in the recent past of his ideas. But the distinction between the fact and value is more important than the distinction between the differing fields of philosophy, religion, literature and so on. There is the job of analysis and then the job of evaluation. I thus consider that the more rational way to deal with belief-systems would be to describe a field which we could designate as worldview analysis, and another, related, field which could be called 'worldview evaluation', including in that the process of worldview construction. I guess that a major task of an original philosopher might well be worldview construction, as it is also of many religious gurus and the like.

I use the word 'worldview' even though it has manifest disadvantages. It has no adjective. It is not altogether a natural word yet in English. It does not sound embodied enough, whereas religion suggests ritual practice and the like. But it is about the best there is in English, and I would suggest that it supplies a missing category in English, as a genus-word to cover both traditionally religious systems of belief and practice and secular systems of a similar nature.[3] It is unfortunate that our language is not all that clear and logical in dealing with beliefs. It is only in modern times that we have really begun to stand back from beliefs and values and afford them a reasonable degree of analysis. In brief, then, I would urge that we bear in mind something wider than religion, namely worldview, and that we should pay special attention to worldview analysis in the educational process.

Let me get at this in a slightly different manner. We know that there are economic and political factors in human existence: and we abstract from the totality of living, breathing human reality in order to analyse those factors. I am merely suggesting that we abstract also the mental factor, in so far as it is expressed in beliefs and values which help to shape society and human activities. In so far as worldviews have their own potency (though often they have little) they are a vital factor in the shaping of civilizations and of groups. And since we all live together in an increasingly intimate global society, it is important that we understand one another's beliefs, whether we find them to be good, bad or indifferent.

It might be remarked that worldview analysis is not, from a philosophical point of view, enough. We surely would not want to give young people the facts about worldviews, both religious and secular, and then simply stand back, without imparting any guidance on the rationality of the views we surveyed. Surely our duty as educators is to give some guidance on the truth.

This itself is a slippery position, hard to hold, tricky to come to grips with. For it is in the nature of worldviews, I think, that their truth is debatable. How do we decide as a matter of educational policy what is right and what is wrong? We may think that Christianity or Scientific Humanism or a bit of both is somehow the truth: but would the Chinese or Iranian authorities concur? And how do we show them to be wrong? Why should it be that education leads to one worldview in one country and another worldview in another country? Or should we regard the young all as world citizens? And then what is the truth for the world as a whole?

Let me digress a little at this point, to consider an important fact about education, whether we are talking of schools or universities. The modern educational system is largely paid for by the State. The typical State is the nation-State: it is therefore

natural that teachers should be expected to inculcate the values
of the nation – the ethics of good citizenship, the myth of national
history and the ideal future, the sentiments of loyalty to the
national group, some of the rituals of national participation, and
the doctrines that underpin the sense of national destiny. The
nation begins to take on the lineaments of a God, and it is a
gracious god, for though it demands dread sacrifices, it also gra-
ciously offers welfare and promises happiness to its citizens. It
often speaks in the language of liberation, and it has often awe-
some powers. So nationalism itself begins to develop into a worldview theme.

A modern State needs education. It needs scientists, social
workers, computer operators, technological designers, engineers,
civil servants. It needs accountants, marketeers, business analysts,
economists, systems persons and managerial trainees. It even, up
to a point, needs humanities folk and anthropologists, though not
too much. It therefore has a bias in regard to truth: it tends
towards conservatism in the humanities, patriotism in history,
and effectiveness in the applied sciences. The State can easily
wish to put truth where its money is.

Now this leads to an observation about decisions concerning
worldviews which is germane to the problem of the criteria of
truth as between them. I shall not now expand on this, but state
my position dogmatically, since I shall be involved in an extended
discussion of the matter later. The observation is that in so far as
pluralism and criticism are what a democratic and open society
should encourage, democratic societies are better able to provide
for modernity and science than are closed societies. But it is a
natural corollary of open debate that the limitations of dogmatism
should be recognized. The position which the democrat should
hold is not a relativistic one, but it is soft. As democrats we
should be soft non-relativists. We should allow that others might
be right. Who can say that Christianity is false because it is
supposedly not rational? What if it be rational to expect worldviews to proceed substantially from symbolic sources? What if it
is rational to expect revelation from the Beyond if God is ever to
address the world that she, having created other than herself, is
hidden behind? And if it is not irrational to believe in God, why
not the Qur'an, why not Islam? Can the Christian prove her
revelation or the Muslim his, over against the other? So it is not

rational to think that there are clear rational answers to the question of the truth of worldviews. I am not denying that the Scientific Humanism that governs so much contemporary philosophical thinking is true. It is just that there are no proofs.

If this is so, then dogmatism is wrong in education. A critical and pluralistic attitude is to be cultivated. There are dangers in dogmatism and especially in the realm of worldviews.

To sum up our thinking so far. First, it is important in trying to describe and re-present the religions and more generally worldviews of others to use bracketing: to try to give a description in other words that brings out the feelings, attitudes, beliefs and meaningful practices of the other. It is so because at the primary and basic level we are concerned with bringing out the nature and power of ideas – whatever we may privately think about their truth. In doing this, we are looking upon religious studies, or more broadly worldview analysis, as historical, social–scientific: we are aiming to present the way things are, or better, the way people are (and have been). It is not our job in this primary stage to judge whether others or ourselves are right or wrong, rational or irrational. At this level it is important educationally, because we live in the new age of a global civilization and of world history. As human beings we need to understand one another. At another level, whether for private aims or for more public reasons, we may ask which worldview is true, rational, most insightful and so on. At this level we need to maintain an open and pluralist posture, in so far as the criteria of truth and so forth are not clear or uncontroversial. By way of corollary, we may state that the present practice in universities is not itself very reasonable, in that the aspectual study of worldviews and religions is typically deeply fragmented.

I began with religious studies and then branched out to worldviews. Let me now revert to speaking primarily of religious studies, and say more about its crucial role in the educational process, even beyond the fact that it has put so centrally upon its agenda the practice of bracketing, the practice of walking in the moccasins of other people. In following its virtues up I shall often be treating of the virtues of others, such as anthropologists and literary folk: for have I not said that the field is multidisciplinary? If I steal the virtues of others, that is intended as a compliment.

The first virtue, beyond bracketing, that I would point to in religion is what may be called obedience to the Contextual

Imperative. It is scarcely right for us to embark upon a history of doctrine or of myth without seeing how those ideas are incarnated and particularized. They are particularized because the broader horizontal context of other doctrines and stories is relevant to the meaning of the doctrine we may be considering. It is quite obvious that the Christian sense of *messiah* differs from the contemporary Jewish one in the years of the formation of the Christian tradition. It is by analogy with the Jewish sense, but it goes from a different reading of the texts of the Hebrew Bible or Old Testament. It is for such reasons that there is a broad dfference between the Hebrew Bible and the Old Testament: I like to say that these are two great books lying at the roots of Western civilization. As for the incarnation of the ideas, it is clear that the myths and emerging doctrines of early Christianity were incarnated in the rituals and practical life of the community. This may be called the 'vertical contextuality' of ideas. It is important to consider the changes which occur to the myths and doctrines themselves as this vertical context changes. But apart from obedience to the Contextual Imperative, the study of religion has the virtue of paying much attention to symbolic forms.

This virtue may be called Symbolic Sensitivity. It is of course impossible for us to take religion seriously without at the same time being involved in attempts to understand the way in which religious symbols work. They are hard to get a handle on: but it is quite obvious that symbols are, so to speak, the vocabulary of mythic thinking. But it is an interesting feature of much contemporary ideology that the rational approach to problems is itself somehow free of mythic and symbolic underpinning. There is a widely shared sense that myths are dead, mere curiosities of the past, and that the truly modern person has rid himself of symbolic forms, except in the arts, where they are carefully kept in a ghetto. It is, of course, characteristic of some religious traditions to dismiss the myths of other traditions as vapid, and to fail to recognize the mythic side of one's own tradition. This is in part why 'myth' has come to mean 'false story' or 'false idea'. We talk now of the myth of progress if we wish to dismiss it, not if we wish to commend it. But in the proper sense, each community bears around a myth about itself, which helps to identify and justify the group. Religious Studies has to be sensitive to such narratives and emotion-laden ideas.

For instance, the very idea that we (whoever we are) have

passed through the Enlightenment and now have emerged into a modern scientific age is itself a myth. It is a myth in the sense of a value-laden narrative. It is a story that lies at the back of many people's minds and which helps to explain attitudes and actions. It is, moreover, a story which has been woven into the fabric of much modern liberal Christianity, and creates tensions with the Biblical worldview, which of course has no sense of the Enlightenment. Incidentally, the very term for this stretch of intellectual history is significant, in view of the various symbolic loadings which the phenomenon of light has almost universally acquired in human thinking.

Symbolic sensitivity is something which is important to education if we are to be aware of the forces playing upon and around us. It helps to humanize the technical. There is a widespread technocratic ideology which sees problems in merely tecnical, not human, terms. But the myths of our time are the more gripping because they are only partially recognized as having mythic qualities: the motorbike, the high-rise apartment building, the Cultural Revolution, the flights to the Moon, the rivalry in intercontinental missiles between the Superpowers, science as a socially incarnate enterprise, tourism – all these are more or less heavily charged concepts or entities, and demand symbolic analysis. It is important that a place be given in the educational process to this enquiry, and a natural place is Religious Studies (another is Anthropology).

Let us give an example: what is the inner meaning of the high-rise apartment block? Typically it is housing created during slum clearance for so-called working class people. It has the property of fulfilling two unrelated aims – of providing a bureaucratic solution to housing needs, and of expressing the arrogant ambition of the modern architect – to scrape heaven. It is born out of Le Corbusier and Chicago. It is modern, rational, impressive.

But is it truly rational? Not if enough people do not want to live in it, so that it has to be pulled down after a couple of decades. Not if it is not cared for, and itself becomes a vertical slum. Not if there is inadequate provision for leisure activities, or if there is no gardening available, and garages, and other civilized facilities. The garden suburb is much nearer to most modern people's desires. And in saying that such an edifice is *modern*, is not something special being meant? It is modern architecturally, namely clean, functional, simple. Never mind if that is not what most people want in their homes. They like decoration, bits of complication, and do not need always to live in the most 'rational' possible mode. What is rational about supplying folk with what is rational if that makes them unhappy, and ill at ease? Deeper in all this perhaps is the following thought: that the highrise apartment building is typically for *them*, for the proletariat. You can drive into virtually any northern European city and tell at a glance where the public housing is. The bureaucrat is also, whether socialist or not, the classifier of people. The apartment building is 'good enough' for those who are classified as suitable to live there. If the elevators get smashed, the stairwells defaced, the entrance halls damaged – these are more than random troubles, but symptoms of alienation.

These are some of the messages conveyed by the highrise. The decipherment of such messages is an important aspect of awareness, and the messages revealed help to form the vocabulary out of which the worldview sentences are constructed. Symbolic Sensitivity is a virtue which reaches out into everyday life.

It by the same token supplies a need for self-analysis. It helps to generate self-awareness about what *my* symbols are. Moreover, Religious Studies, because it demands that we use the method of *epoche*, of bracketing our own beliefs and values, demands of us an account of what those beliefs and values are. The analysis of others demands the analysis of one's self. There is no word for this: it is somewhat analogous to psychoanalysis, but it is more analysing emotions and beliefs, not from a problematic, but from a descriptive, point of view. It is an analysis of our attitudes, truly of our soul, but we cannot call it depth analysis, since that notion has already been taken over by psychiatry and psychoanalysis. It is, if one were to coin a phrase, noo-analysis. From one point of view it does not matter what you believe, provided that you know what it is that you believe. So Symbolic Sensitivity implies some degree of what I shall call 'Noo-Analytic Awareness'.

That itself implies a degree of self-criticism and critical posture which of course fits in with the openness of enquiry which seems to be demanded both by scholarship and by science.

Critical analysis will suggest that we tend to live in a certain amount of *aporia*. Do we, when it comes to the crunch, really have a systematic worldview? We have an amalgam of beliefs, which we may publicly characterize in a certain way. I may *say* that I am an Episcopalian, but how much of my real worldview corresponds to the more or less official views of the Episcopal Church? How much is in any case left out by an 'official world-view' which tells me nothing directly about cricket, being Scottish, having a certain scepticism about nationalism, thinking that there is life on other worlds, shelving the problem of evil or other matters. Our values and beliefs are more like a collage than a Canaletto. They do not even have consistency of perspective.

There is growing realization of this untidiness at the public level also, in the contemporary growth of Religious Studies. More scholars are turning to regional studies, particular contexts, anthropological domains: it is not Christianity, but Catholicism we need to look at; not Catholicism but Spanish; not Spanish but in North Eastern Spain; not North Eastern but a particular county; not a county but a village. Such studies help to multiply our sense of the pluralism of Christianity itself. They also help to reinforce the thought that there is no pure instantiation of a faith: such essences as may be propounded turn out at best very rough approximations, but more likely they are normative expressions of how the speaker feels how the faith ought to be.

So Religious Studies ought to generate in us a healthy feeling for what may be called 'Syncretistic Realism' – the fact that any religious or worldview movement has an ideology which is a mixture of things. There is no Calvinism in Scotland, but there is Scottish Calvinism (or there was!). It is such blends of worldview themes (the national theme, the tradition theme) that typically go to make up actual worldviews. This is sometimes denied from an ideal point of view: the Scottish Calvinism may not see the Scottishness as essential. But the fact of blending is everywhere to behold: Iranian nationalism and Shi'i revival; liberal evolutionism and Lutheranism in pre-World War II German Protestantism; American values and robust right-wing Evangelicalism in the Moral Majority; and so on. These descriptions are, of course, crude in the extreme. Actual collages are much more complicated. To unravel contemporary Iranian Nationalism, for instance, one would have to pay attention to ideas about modernization (not rejected, despite the anti-Western trends of Iranian propaganda), of Khomeini's updating of Islamic law in his writings, and many other things besides. So I think that our studies can generate a sense of 'Syncretistic Realism' in the analysis of sets of powerful ideas. It then becomes a further analysis to see how far we can identify the strong symbolic motifs which cause a collage to be dynamic, or the other strong political and economic forces which may come to dominate the collage.

It may well be remarked that Syncretistic Realism is something which is well-known in the history of ideas: there is nothing so special about Religous Studies in all this. Well, I did promise to steal virtues. But there is a strand, a feeling, a combination which the history of ideas has had less to do with: the collages with which we are concerned are not just ideas. They are not just sets of doctrines and legal or ethical precepts: though they in fact include these. They are symbolic constructions, and are capable of moving people, and of bridging the gap between feeling and reality which human beings need to cross. It is, then, the combination between the virtues of Symbolic Sensitivity and Syncretistic Realism, both applied according to the canons of the Contextual Imperative, that needs to be emphasized. It is not a combination unique to Religious Studies, but it is central to its operations.

These virtues, together with the central concern with walking in other people's moccasins – with structured empathy – give Religious Studies a crucial place in that wider enterprise which may be dubbed worldview analysis. And worldview analysis supposes in turn that ideas as moving people are important to treat of in human history and in contemporary understanding. It generates a philosophy which modifies prevalent 'materialistic' attitudes. By these I mean a mixture of ordinary attitudes and quasi-philosophical attitides: the view that the real determinants of action are cash and fear, or that the underlying economic and class structure is what counts in generating ideological attitudes, which themselves have a very weak effect in the evolution of the structure that gives rise to them, or that human beings will act rationally if they are allowed to, and this means acting in conformity with the principles of scientific humanism. Such a cluster of ideas underestimates ideals; it undervalues human beings' courage and recklessness when grippped by causes, and undervalues existential problems of identity, and therefore nationalism and other forces counterposed to the principles which 'rational' people will espouse. If this is a thumbnail sketch of prevalent attitudes which do not give scope to the power of ideas and symbolic values, then we need to take note: for such attitudes are not truly realistic, though they pretend to be just that. They are

attitudes which are embedded in contemporary analytic philosophy, in most forms of Marxism, in technological humanism,
and among hard-headed exponents of economic rationalism. They
are attitudes which fall into the greatest fallacy of contemporary
times: the view that because certain things are untrue, or useless
for me, or irrational, or not practical, therefore they are unimportant for others and have no purchase on the world. They
represent that old ideological weakness: the underestimation of
the Other.

So far I have argued for Religious Studies, and more broadly
for Worldview Analysis, on intellectual grounds, for the most
part. But let me add a few obvious considerations, which I shall
expand upon later, which relate to our own and most other
Western societies. First, there are important minority populations
which traditionally practise different religions from mainstream
Christianities such as have proved dominant hitherto in Western
cultures. Second, there are important minorities which have old
roots in Western cultures but which have in the past been
neglected or worse by prevalent ideologues and educationalists –
most notably Judaism. Third, we need for both practical and
other reasons to have a better understanding in the old imperial
heartlands of so-called Third World cultures. Fourth, young people especially but all people in principle now have wide existential
choices in lifestyle, and so need to understand something about
alternative lifestyles. Fifth, new religions sprout, and add to the
complexity of our worldview situation in the West. For these and
no doubt other reasons it is important that we should have at our
disposal educationally the resources to deal with the world's
pluralism.

But what do we find? There is often a powerful lobby, taking
differing forms in differing countries, which urges the teaching
of Christian values in the school system: often this means some
kind of Biblical Christianity, which is to be imposed upon young
people of different backgrounds (or if not, they can be excused
from instruction). We have in the United Kingdom a still dominant place in universities of a kind of ecumenical–Protestant kind
of theology as the norm. In most Western countries there is,
nevertheless – or perhaps I might say because of this – still strong
suspicion of the study of religion, fearing that it may turn out to
be tertiary Sunday School. The atheists, rationalists and Marxists
are often opposed to the teaching of religion, either for fear of

indoctrination or because no encouragement to irrational views should be given. In philosophy departments typically a sophisticated version of humanism is presented, as the worldview which thoughtful people should have: so that philosophy while obviously containing some merely analytical and educational elements also is seen somehow as the successor of theology, as presenting civilization's most well articulated ideology.

In these and other ways that form of intellectual endeavour which is aimed at defending, articulating or constructing a worldview – what may be called the presentational rather than the representational approach to beliefs – can often tend against pluralism of exposition. It can easily be the enemy of a rich crosscultural approach to Religious Studies and worldview analysis.

I say all this without opposing Christian theology, or philosophical humanism as such. I follow a version of Christianity, and I have taught happily in philosophy departments in the UK and the United States. So it is not to undervalue these activities that I write; but rather to protest against tendencies to exclusivism. There is neither a God-given nor a humanity-bestowed right to teach a debatable worldview as though it is not debatable, nor to neglect the deeply held beliefs and values of other people on the ground that you consider them foolish. But it is often the foolish beliefs that turn out to be dynamic, for good or ill: and by what criteria do we judge alternative worldviews to be irrational? So I am only arguing against, not philosophy, but some philosophers' restrictions upon pluralism; not Christian theology, but against those who do not have a generous view of alternative religious outlooks. There are, of course, serious political implications of the position I have adopted and these in turn will have repercussions on education. But of all that, more anon.

So far I have given prominence to the process of understanding worldviews. The emphasis has been upon empathetic description, upon histories, upon the delineation of the various ideal forces at work. But I have not said much about two directions in which Religious Studies is pulled, beyond just descriptions. One direction is towards theory, and the other towards judgment of truth and value.

In regard to the latter direction, we are in this drawn towards the philosophy of religion, or should it be better called 'the philosophy of worldviews'? We are drawn, that is, towards the exploration of the criteria by which we may judge as to the fruits and truth of religous systems. This enquiry is still in its infancy, for philosophers of religion still to a great extent concentrate on issues internal to theism and to the Western tradition, whereas the choices are, of course, world wide. Later, we shall discuss some of the issues here in so far as they bear on education. But it seems obvious, as we have already argued, that there can be no proofs from one worldview to another, or between worldviews. Religious and other worldviews are flexible, sinuous and capable of adaptation, which is why it is hard to falsify a position con-clusively. They often seem like a series of concurrent paradigms, so that one looks implausible from the perspective of another, and conversely. They are held often with certainty, but the feeling which surrounds them must be one of doubt. The criteria of truth and value do not vanish altogether, but they undoubtedly soften. And if this be so as a philosophical judgment then it would seem to follow that toleration becomes a virtue. The natural outcome of pluralistic philosophy of worldviews is a tolerant attitude. This at a higher level no doubt can itself become a criterion: intolerant and over-dogmatic systems will be thought unfortunate and dangerous. But generally speaking, the attitude arising will be not only tolerant but tending too towards a kind of pan-religious ecumenism. It would not be unreasonable to see openness to alternative views as part of that very pluralism which is a pre-supposition, as we saw, of democratic education. Indeed, the study of worldviews in a tolerant and analytical manner would be a sign of democratic ideology, and a distinguishing feature of democratic over against alternative worldviews.

This factor, incidentally, can be cited as a reason against objec-tivity or impartiality. Is there not already this bias built into the comparative study of religion? Is it not correct after all that comparative religion makes people comparatively religious? It may be so, though I would put it differently ('Crosscultural study makes people crossculturally religious'): but the point about bracketing and the use of imagination is that fanaticism itself becomes something to enter into. The crosscultural student of religious and other worldviews is still immeasurably better off in regard to understanding than is the monocultural navel-watcher.

As for the theoretical side of the study of religion, probably the least interesting are those wideranging reductionisms that deal holistically with the genesis of religion. More to the point is that students of religion need a vocabulary of symbolic and other forms, a syntax of how they are used in systems, a theory of change, and so on. To a considerable extent elements of a complex and wideranging theory of religion are already in place: the vocabulary of symbolism in part is supplied by Eliade, part of the syntax by philosophical analysis, some of the theory of change by Weber. We can see the beginnings of a dynamic phenomenology to replace the more static typology pioneeered by van der Leeuw. Already, the field has been greatly enriched, especially over the last twenty-five years by many fine historical studies of different traditions and regions of the globe. The possibility of using a dimensional analysis of religion to frame theories of how changes in one dimension, e.g. religious experience, affect what occurs in other dimensions, e.g. doctrine, will become more important as we seek a more organic, yet dynamic, mode of seeing intra-religious explanations. All these aspects of theory in religion – and more generally worldviews – suggest that we can show a logic in interplays and changes which is not itself revealed by the religion or worldview itself. In other words, we shall supply, and are already to some extent supplying, historical and sociological and phenomenological modes of explaining change and structure in religion which are not derived from the teachings of any religion, but belong rather to that human science of religion which the field of worldview analysis helps to construct.

This divergence between theological, ideological or pious accounts and the more theoretical explanations deriving from the new study of religion is an instance of that modern self-consciousness which has affected the human sciences. The fact that we do not just practise religion or ideology, but study it means a new phase of human awareness. It involves a revolution in thinking and feeling: we can no longer feel or think something, but we almost automatically need to reflect about it, and that begins to alter our reactions and perceptions. I often think about this in the following terms.

My favourite miracle in the New Testament is Jesus's first, at a wedding in Cana in Galilee, when he turned about 150 gallons of water into wine. The scale of what he did never ceases to amaze me. I hear the passage read, on the relevant Sunday, in church, and my mind begins to shoot in various directions. Should we read it as a parable? Obviously that is attractive because I can't believe it really happened. Of course, the words wash over me, the scene is fixed in my imagination, I am absorbed by a scene which lights up as it were before my very eyes. But I do not believe it. I am not gripped by the mythic milieu, the sacred presentation, the narrative certainty. I am a 'modern' person, and I cannot seriously believe in the miracle (though I do believe in miracles of healing and the like). So I am condemned to reflect as I hear it, and before you know what has happened I am in a deep reverie about mythic thinking, sacred narratives, parables. And it is this sort of self-consciousness which is indeed the contemporary condition, now that the philosophy and theory of worldviews has come to roost in our souls. Pure belief is no longer possible. It is not enough to affirm something: one must have a view about the criteria of affirmation. It is not enough to believe something, but one must have a view about the epistemology of belief. It is not enough to think something: one must have at the same time a notion of where what we think fits into the global picture. It is in these ways that we are 'modern', and all children of Proust. It is as if we all now need to go around with looking glasses in our pockets, or in our purses. Many of us do anyway, thus symbolizing our mental condition.

Yet it is strange that all the time the analysis of worldviews, which we should as far as is in us conduct in as impartial a manner as possible, and which we should permeate with the spirit of inward objectivity and informed empathy, keeps nudging us in a particular direction. It keeps reminding us of the need for toleration and openness. It rests upon the thought that facts about people are after all facts, and about what is or is not the case a free environment is advisable, so that we can rid ourselves of pressures to distort reality. The pursuit nudges us towards a system where individual freedom is prized, the right to dissent is protected, ideological conformity is not insisted upon and openness and toleration are prized. The very pursuit of worldview analysis and of the modern study of religion seems to commit us to a sort of politics, and to a sort of worldview. It is true that democratic individualism is not Buddhist, Christian or Jewish: but it is not in any orthodox way Marxism and it can run counter to the forces of nationalism. I accept these implications. It is true that our study is not possible in a large number of countries and social systems. It would be hard in the Sudan, impossible in Pakistan, difficult in Tunisia, misunderstood in Yugoslavia, banned in the Soviet Union, and so on. It is not very easy in the Western world. But it has the future, I hope, on its side. The logic of education and of scientific discovery underpins it. If it is hard to achieve it is because human beings are often conservative, and so easily think in the out-of-date categories of their childhood and upbringing.

One final thought in regard to Religious Studies and the Western mind. Its shape does indeed look Western, but the concepts which we shall use in studying religions and worldviews will be increasingly eclectic and crosscultural in character. And will there not be increasing call for more than national accounts of where we are? Will education across the world not increasingly call for accounts that are indeed global? Will not world history, world literature, world religions become the necessary stuff of education as time goes on? Yes, we shall still have Scottish and Armenian and American history, but seen in a wider whole; and not just the analysis and presentation of Scottish and Armenian and American values, but values that are somehow universally human? I think it is inevitable. This is not to say that there will not be backlashes, retreats into older narrower forms, strikes towards revolutionary particularity, demands for being left alone culturally. But all that will be within the wider context which often seems so threatening to the particular and for that reason stirs the backlashes.

Now if that wider view will be called for, it means that students in schools and colleges will be asked to read world histories. And it is important for us to ask what those histories will contain. For if it is by British history that the British attain a consciousness of being British, and by French history French and so on, then it is by human history as a whole that young people will attain a sense of being human, that is members of a common human family. But *how* they will experience that will depend upon the kind of books that are written for them, and that in turn will rest upon the kind of scholarly attitudes that are cultivated in our universities. What I have been insisting on, from different directions, is that a vital aspect of global studies is the mental geography of the world, and the history of that geography.

For we are only incompletely prepared if we only know about rocks, and earthquakes, and oceans, and rivers and savannah and coal. We also need to know about Christs, and Buddhas, and Marxes, and selflessness and the Trinity and the Tao and African classical categories and the not so distant sounds of the minaret.

2

The Political Implications of Religious Studies

There used to be a model of the study of religion which in different parts of the world still persists somewhat, and that is the view that the primary purpose in studying a religion is to practise it, and that the main consequence of advanced study is theological expertise. This model is the traditional Christian theological one; in other forms it is to be found in Judaism, Islam and elsewhere. It assumes the truth of a given religious tradition or subtradition, and it believes that citizens' children and citizens themselves should be exposed to those ideas. It tends to think that the State is justified in using the money gained from taxpayers to pay the salaries of those who teach the tradition or subtradition in question. It is a model which has and still has immense influence upon humanity. Moreover, if we extend the study of religion to the study of secular worldviews it may stimulate us to reflect that the same situation prevails, secularly, in Marxist countries: a main job of schools and universities is to train people in scientific atheism and to drill them in the values of the Marxist tradition. Somewhat similar things may happen in rightwing countries too, where some local ideology will be *de rigueur*.

This model of theology and religious education may be generous-minded. It may allow that minorities, such as Jews, can withdraw from school lessons. Provisions may be made for Jewish higher education. It may be too that in some part of the theological faculty provision is made for the study of world religions other than the predominating one.

It is obvious that this model cannot stand up to the arguments for pluralistic study contained in my previous chapter. But the idea that we have a certain set of values which need in education to be handed on is a strong one. It is not it would seem unreasonable to set forth and transmit something of the tradition which has formed us. If we have a Christian heritage, then we should pass on the Christian faith as the norm. Such is the sentiment which lies behind the older model which underpins so much in education and theology in our schools and universities. But the model is fallacious – and indeed pernicious – and it has origins which should remind us of the ways in which it has fostered the oppression of minorities and even in many cases majorities.

The model is a hangover from the principle of *cuius regio eius religio*: citizens need to follow the religious commitment of the ruler, or in different terms citizens should obey the religious and ideological dictates of the government. The model depends upon the principle of established religion, or more generally of established worldview. In my opinion there should be no established worldview other than that implied in the doctrine that there should be no established worldview. The sooner our citizens are educated in this the better. Moreover, such a pluralistic principle is in accord not only with the spirit of the university but also with the new realities of our citizenry, which is drawn from many countries as well as the prevailing group, and which also espouses, even in the prevailing group, quite a number of different beliefs and non-beliefs, and of varying practises.

It may be replied that probably the majority approves of universal Christian religious education, and would be quite happy to have Anglican or Presbyterian divines in theological posts in Glasgow or Oxford. Even if the majority thinks that Christian religious education makes people into better citizens and better human beings, this is by itself no argument. The majority can tyrannize. One of the stupidest concepts of modern political life is that democracy consists somehow in majority rule. The only way in which majority rule where the minority is tyrannized is better than minority rule where the majority is tyrannized lies in numbers. The truly free country is one where the minorities have rights too. Moreover, the fact that the majority may believe that Christian education produces better citizens is fairly irrelevant, in that the majority can be wrong in any event in its judgments. Also, by the way, being a good citizen is not the highest state: the good citizen is taught to give up part of his wealth, and some of this goes to manufacturing arms with which to kill non-citizens. Citizens that do not follow government orders to kill non-citizens are deemed disloyal, and may themselves be killed. I am not saying that there are not just wars: but only that being a loyal citizen of a modern nation-State is not the highest ideal.

The idea of *cuius regio, eius religio* derives from an old thought, or rather from two old thoughts. One is the authority of the ruler: the other is that there has to be agreement in worldview for citizens who are joined together in a common State. The second principle is usually interpreted to mean 'a substantive worldview'. Kings debated whether to adopt Christianity or Islam, or Catholicism or Protestantism, or to stay with Yggdrasil or look instead to the Cross of Christ. They adopted Buddhism or Hindu cosmology as a means of rule; or Confucianism or State Shinto . . . and so on. In Britain it turned out that the State religions rather sloppily, but excellently for the times, varied: the Welsh, with their 18th and 19th century Non-Conformism, and the Irish with their stubborn Catholicism, rebelled against official ideas. But the apparatus of a State religion in Britain, though much of it remains in place, is inappropriate, and this should have strong social, political and educational consequences, to which I shall come.

The United States of course has constitutional principles running in the opposite direction. It is true that priests and rabbis may say prayers at Inaugurations of Presidents: there is what Bellah has called America's civil religion.[1] But there is at the same time a ban on using taxpayers' money to subsidize chairs of theology or to finance the teaching of any one religion in school. It is constitutional to teach about religions, but unconstitutional to teach a particular religion, in the public school system. Of course pluralism allows private schools and private universities. If Harvard wants to have a Divinity School it can have one, and it can treat the teaching of world religions as an element in its operation. But the public system, both higher and lower, has been chary of any religious studies. Thus in the University of California, all campuses have departments or programs of philosophy, but only a minority have Religious Studies, and only one campus, Santa Barbara, has a fully fledged Department offering doctoral work. There are other State Universites which have no teaching of Religious Studies. The vast majority of schools have nothing on religion, save some historical scraps falling by the wayside of social studies. This leads to an irony in my life: in Britain I fight for pluralism against the assumption of Christianity; in the United States against the assumption of nothing.

If the United States constitution is the chief counterexample of the *cuius regio* principle, the chief exponents of the doctrine in modern times are less the rather enfeebled establishmentarianism of Scotland or Sweden, but rather the Marxist countries. Only we would now need perhaps to re-translate it, as 'Of whom the rule, of him the ideology' – *cuius regio, eius ideologia* or *cuius regio, eius philosophia*. This incidentally is where the question of the definition of religion becomes of great importance. Had Communism been treated as a religion or quasi-religion, it would have been hard for McCarthyism to maintain its impetus. Once we think in terms of worldviews, rather than something rather narrowly conceived of as religion, the applications of the rules begin to change in a very heady fashion.

This, by the way, might lead us to view the distinction betwen religion and the secular as itself an ideological distinction.[2] It draws the line a particular way which suits modern society, e.g. in regard to taxation, the definition of a charity, and so forth. It separates out religion and in some degree thereby tames it. Religion is assumed often to be a 'private' matter, and not something that can rightly enter into the main substance of politics. If the narrower definition of religion, distinguishing it from secular worldviews, is indeed an ideologically determined choice, then it needs to be treated with scepticism. But there are plenty of other grounds for not accepting a narrow way of looking at religious worldviews as if they were *toto coelo* differentiated from secular ones, as we have seen.

All this suggests that in a pluralist and democratic society, no worldview-affirming institution (no church in a very broad sense) should be officially adopted by the State. No citizen should be disadvantaged for holding to one worldview rather than another. As I have remarked, it is the Marxist countries which are now the chief exponents of the old principle, and it means that citizens are disadvantaged for not belonging to or affirming support for the official worldview-affirming institution, namely the Communist Party of the relevant country. Citizens may be disadvantaged for other reasons, e.g. being part of the left-over bourgeoisie, or for ethnic reasons, but primarily it is disloyalty to the *credo* of the rulers that brings problems, ranging from prisons and torture to lack of oportunities and advancement. Such States can claim to have religious freedom but this is not the same as worldview-freedom, even where practise of cults is relatively open. So from the vantage-point of Marxist orthodoxy, again, the narrower treatment of religion as in a separate categorial basket from secular worldviews has a certain advantage. We may note that in such States there is forbidden the teaching of religion; State schools, which are the only ones, must teach scientific socialism; and to all intents there is official worldview-transmission.

The radical alternative to this is to have a pluralistic curriculum, in which various worldviews are presented (in principle, all the main worldviews of the world), and in which none is seen as the 'official' view: leaving choice openly to the students and citizens.

But it will be objected that this radical alternative is not after all so radical: does it not itself imply a worldview? And so is it not merely masquerading as an alternative path? It is really the same idea, but presented in a more genteel and bourgeois and Western fashion. I think we need to investigate to see that it is in the way of a worldview which the pluralistic alternative implies.

First, it implies an epistemology. It implies that there are no absolutely clearcut ways of proving one religion over another or one worldview over another. This soft epistemology implies that worldviews are, from the angle of criteria and proofs, opinion. Where opinions predominate then the educationalist points to the alternatives; and the democrat allows for divergences of belief in society. Only where there is proof would one be justified in teaching anything with certainty as the truth, the 'received opinion'.

In other words, a soft epistemology implies toleration. But there is more than softness: there is productivity lying behind the notion that we should have an open society. Knowledge advances by imaginative exploration and criticism – not taking any position as established, probing and seeking weak spots. This is the epistemology of Karl Popper. It claims that the open society, in encouraging criticism and debate, is a better engine for the production of new knowledge than is the closed society. But we cannot arbitrarily restrict enquiry, for instance by thinking of worldviews as not open to debate, but of scientific hypotheses or literary judgments as so open. So a society open in one way will need ultimately to be open in all. And this entails pluralism.

But liberty is not simply something instrumental to greater knowledge, important as that may be. It is something to which individuals and groups have a right (the democrat may think), provided that in the exercise of that right they do not infringe the liberty of others. Now this principle, which I believe is that which in Western democracies we all at least pay lip service to, allows great variation of practice, but it does pull some of the teeth of the worldviews whose practice it makes room for. It is a tame Islam or Catholicism or Marxism that it may allow: it is Islam without Islamic society, Marxism without Marxist revolution, Catholicism with limited sway for the Pope. For how could a pluralistic democratic society agree to the Shari'sa as the law of the land, or to Leninist secret police, or to Papal dictates about censorship? So the Muslims, Marxists and Catholics who operate in a democratic society do seem to have their teeth pulled. But this does not mean that they do not have real freedoms in such a society.

The Muslim has the freedom not to eat pork, to arrange marriage in accord with Islamic law, to worship at his mosque, to pray daily, to go to Mecca. It is true that there are some restrictions on the full implementation of Muslim law, but he does have a large measure of traditional Islamic activity open to him. He will have more freedom than would a Bahai under Islamic law. So there is at least in principle a maximization of pluralism, to the greatest degree possible, that is, for one group in relation to the susceptibilities of other groups.

But all this is based upon a doctrine of human rights, and why should we accept *that*? This is where we return to the questions of epistemology. Only if you can be sure that something is wrong are you entitled to prevent someone else from doing it. Now some rules, against murder, stealing, lying, for instance, are necessary for the existence of any society, and so we need to obey them. But lots of other rules, about eating pork, marriage, homosexuality, etc., do not have this necessary status, and can be left as matters of 'opinion'. Moreover some issues, such as abortion, have ambiguous status for there are problems generated by conflict of rules. I would say that about a variety of religious and other practices we cannot, in the public arena, be sure. So these rules cannot be taught as certain nor imposed upon others. As a Muslim I may be against the sale of alcohol, but it is wrong to impose it upon all. But people are entitled to hold for themselves views and precepts which are deeply held. I would think, incidentally, in a pluralistic society there could be accommodation over such rules as marriage. Why should a Muslim in a pluralistic society not fully follow traditional Islamic marriage law, provided there is protection of the rights of women?

But this appeal to the softness of the epistemology is not going to be very agreeable to dedicated Muslims, Buddhists, Christians, Atheists, Marxists and so on. Will they not by definiton be sure of what their faith entails?

They are in one sense of 'sure' entitled to be sure of whatever it is that they are committed to; but this certitude is different from public certainty. If I may use the word 'certitude' for subjective sureness, and 'certainty' for public sureness; or if you prefer it 'certitude' for private commitment and 'certainty' for public provability; then, we need to distinguish between the epistemological softness as a publc matter, and private conviction. I may be sure that Geronimo is going to win the 2.30, but I have no right to erect that into a public fact before the event. As far as others are concerned it is just an opinion that he is going to win. It is ludicrous to suppose that there is a public proof of the truth of Christianity or of atheism. Those who have thought that there was such public proof have done much harm, in trying to force obedience to what should have been presented as opinion. There was no justification for the Inquisition, or for Luther's Biblical castigation of the Jews.

But does all this represent a worldview? Does pluralistic openness itself constitute a worldview? I would say not; but it does represent a theme in the spirit of the modern world, mainly since the Enlightenment. As such a theme it might be held to be a worldview-theme, if not by itself a fully fledged worldview. It is higher-order in basis, but it does have lower-order consequences.

Let me then admit that it is at least a thematic element which worldviews need to take account of. As a worldview-theme it may, despite being second-order, have that degree of softness in epistemology which we associate with other worldviews. But it is a powerful theme, and one that religious and secular traditions need to take seriously, and so try to work into the fabric of their own beliefs. In fact there are forms of liberal Christianity, Judaism, Islam, Buddhism and so forth which work pluralism into their schemes of belief and practice. In fact, liberal protestant Christianity was the main pioneer of liberal religion in modern times. It has been followed, through the aftermath of Vatican II, by the Roman Catholic Church, which now incorporates heady drafts of liberalism within its softening structure. It has been expressed well in liberal Judaism in America and elsewhere.

But, it may be replied, if liberal worldviews are best, they cannot be proved to be so. They fall under the rubric of epistemological softness like every other worldview. It may be so. But let me just add a point which in this context in which we are speaking and hearing, reading and writing is significant. There is the context of the university. The university institution as we understand it is one dedicated to the pursuit of truth, and it is in its internal nature as such dedicated to the epistemology which brings truth. It should be host to criticism and debate. It should be open and plural. Largely, modern universities do have this character. It is no coincidence that it was Lancaster, a new university, which advertized its Chair of Religious Studies as open to someone 'of any faith or none'. Sir Charles Carter, the first Vice-Chancellor, sometimes quipped that I was Professor of Any Faith or None. It is not that universities always strictly follow the principle of openness. Schools of thought develop and take over Departments or whole disciplines. But it is surely impossible for a university to deny the principle of pluralism, of open enquiry. So even if such a worldview theme cannot in general be proved, it has certainty within the commitments of the university.

There are of course matters of emphasis. Chinese should no doubt do more work on Chinese history and literature, Russians on Russian, Scotsmen on Scots, and so forth. No doubt a Christian country will harbour more studies of Christianity than will a Buddhist country, which in turn will have some emphasis on Buddhism. But neither country would be right in shutting out alternatives from its educational system.

There will be those who say or think: But learning about Buddhism will confuse the young, and might draw them away from the Christian faith. What pitiful thinking! If the young are confused they have a right to be: it is a confusing world; and if the presentation of Buddhism makes Christianity seem less certain, so be it – it does, in one sense. Surely the Christian faith is strong enough to see Buddhist virtues and learn from them: it does not need the spurious shield of concealment in order to maintain its vigour.

It would seem from these remarks that I am treating university and schools on a par. I am by implication urging pluralism in the high schools, in the primary schools even. That is right. I see no reason why a subject should be in principle different at school level from what it is at university level. The degree of attainment will of course differ. The complexity of conceptual apparatus will be a good deal less at primary school than at high school or at college. But I see no special reason to think that we have some different *subject* at school from what we have at the university, and so the same principles ought to apply. If openness and pluralism are important at university why should they not be so in our schools?

There is a major point that needs to be put in parenthesis here. It happens that the teaching of Christianity in a non-pluralist tradition is hopeless and narrowly conceived. It has been common in Britain and some other countries to concentrate the teaching of Christianity on learning from the Bible. The reason for this is that at least differing Christians from diverse traditions can agree upon the importance of the Bible. There is also a very heavy emphasis upon Biblical enquiry in theological schools in universities and elsewhere. Now I am not one to say that the Bible is not important for Christians; but it is ludicrous as a source for learning about Christian life and Christian pratice, especially in the school context. In most Christian denominations the Bible is read in church: it is interpreted: it is woven into the very fabric of Christian living. Maybe it is the bones of Christianity, and the sacramental and spiritual life is the flesh. What is happening is that the Bible is plucked from its usual living context, and treated as a textbook.

More relevantly one would teach Christianity through a variety of living and historical examples, and no doubt the Bible would have to appear somewhat there, for it was precious to many Christians. Similarly it is best to treat of Buddhism by looking at the various dimensions: ritual, experience, institutions, stories, teachings, ethics, art. Through the lens of Theravadin Buddhism in Sri Lanka one could look back upon the texts of Buddhism. But it would be absurd to judge the whole of Buddhism by the texts.

The notion that it is best to teach the Bible because Christians agree upon the Bible also imports the wrong judges. The clergy are of course vital to the faith: but they are not as such educationalists and they are in fact nearer to being the living data than the teachers about those data. If Christians disagree about a lot of things that is something which the young need to know.

It will show them that there are Christianities not a monolithic Christianity. If dispute between Christians is a bad thing (and I suspect some of it is, though some of it is not), then that is relevant to their judgment about the truth of the faith. They should look at it, warts and all. If they fall in love it will be despite some of the warts. So a better-fleshed treatment of Christianity is called for. But because chairs and syllabuses have been created in the past in the context of seminary-type training, and because ministers and priests need to be able to preach from texts, an excessive investment in Biblical Christianity is to be found in our universities, and far too little of the rich variety of forms of Christian spirituality. But all that is an aside.

The chief conclusion my argument comes to is that we ought to have education in plural worldview analysis in the schools, colleges and universities. Young people ought to learn about the mental geography of our planet, as well as the mental geography of their own country or region. But this is based upon a political principle, that there should be no established worldview-institution, whether church, mosque or party.

The natural drift of this is towards individualism: let the individual choose her worldview, her commitment. This is because the pluralism exhibits more nakedly the breakdown of authority. If there are real alternatives to the Pope, then loyalty to the Pope becomes elective. He is chosen, and he does not choose. So there is in the very process of crosscultural study an erosion of traditionally conceived authorities. But such erosion often leads to backlashes. In fact, if we conceive of the cultural complex which gives rise to emphathetic worldview analysis as a separate tradition, then when other traditions meet it, something occurs which is typical of the wider world, where traditions meet. A meets B and each affects the other, so that we get Ab and Ba. But this can generate a backlash. We get Aa and Bb. So in this sort of way you get a kind of traditionalist backlash, which at one level was represented in the writings of Karl Barth (other religions became quite irrelevant to the revelation of God in Christ); and at a cruder Biblical level in the teachings of the so-called fundamentalist Christians.[3]

The question to be posed here is whether those who at least in overt ideology are not individualists, who affirm the authority of scripture with great vehemence, who wish to create new Christian communities in a state of uncritical solidarity, can be coped with happily enough in my version of disestablishment? Can the more individualistic philosophy which I have presented deal with more collectivist and authoritarian views? I think so: for pluralism implies toleration for groups as well as individuals. If individuals give up their freedom to choose, by joining a sect, so be it. If Muslims or Buddhists wish to continue their religious and cultural customs, that in itself presents no problem. The only real condition attaching to such peaceful coexistence is that conversion be by persuasion and that the general, necessary rules of society be observed.

The individualism which tends to flow out of the pluralistic ethos is a rich individualism. It is not the restricted individualism of rationalist liberals and the classic libertarians. That is, it is an individualism which stresses the importance of groups and traditions. It wishes to walk in many moccasins: the green ones of Islam, the saffron ones of Buddhism, the royal blue ones of Eastern Orthodox Christianity. It wishes that such traditions maintain a degree of vigour, to increase human choice and insight. It does not demand that the individual have no family. It does not despise pedigrees and histories and mythic belonging. It loves what humans love, even when humans do not love individualism. It does not say that the human being need be alone. But it does say that the individual in the last resort makes a choice. If he does not like Catholicism after all, let him walk out. If she does not like purdah, let her cast off the veil. If she does not believe in humanism any longer, let her join a Church. And so on.

Does all this mean that the truth of worldviews is irrelevant? Does it mean that in the grey night of individualism all the cats of belief are equally grey? No: there is no need to assume that everyone is right, only that everyone has a right to be wrong. The varying sects and denominations and movements and churches and religions are all there with something to offer: without it they would scarcely survive. So I have no doubt that there is some truth or value in everything. But there are bad things too. It is for us to provide an education which at least helps the young to make up their minds about these things. They must become as far as possible *religiate*, worldview-sensitive. So there is no need to conclude with indifferentism or relativism. There are criteria of truth; but they are, we must recall, soft criteria. So we have to see at least darker and lighter shades of grey.

The rich individualism which flows from the pluralistic viewpoint allows, then, for crosscultural empathy. In principle it embraces the whole of human civilization as we know it today. It provides at the same time the groundwork for a critical view of one's own tradition and national culture. It appreciates traditions, but it has some explosive things to say about our own society. For one thing, it means disestablishment seriously.

In Britain the most serious educational entrenchments of religion or worldview probably lie in the theological faculties and departments. It is true that the number of Chairs explicitly tied to clerical appointments is diminishing, and is not now great. But it is no coincidence that the great majority of chairholders have been Anglican clergymen, in England, and Presbyterian clergy in Scotland. The position in England is more significant for many departments of theology are in civic or what might be called 'state' universities, outside of the traditional faculties of divinity, whereas in Scotland all posts styled 'theology' or 'divinity' are in traditional faculties. In other words, the Anglican or more broadly the ecumenical establishment moved out from Oxbridge after World War II and happily ensconced itself in the new departments of theology which were being formed or expanded up and down England.

Now it is true that in a pragmatic way the departments of theology began to accommodate a more plural perspective; but keeping the name 'theology' was itself of some moment. To use the term without a prefix (actually people studied Christian, not Jewish or Islamic theology, except for a touch of Buber and Ibn Rushd), was to affirm that there is such an academic study – as if God were there, pure and undefined, waiting like the moon to be an object of study. Without prefix the subject is fraudulent: with a prefix it is egregiously particular, and cries out for pluralism. So although many fine things go on in theology departments and though I myself sometimes practice Christian theology, I would argue that the notion of theology *tout court* is inappropriate to our times, and represents a neat way of affirming a kind of ecumenical establishmentarianism.

Mind you, all this is a small matter. So many ways of arranging academic divisions are irrational. But of course it is symptomatic of a much larger question. If we cannot legitimately talk about 'theology' *tout court* it implies a recognition of alternatives that would make an established religion also inappropriate. So let us be clear, that the very pluralism implied in the conception of Religious Studies or of Worldview Analysis itself drives us towards a radical political view, namely that no one symbol or set of doctrines is adequate to the beliefs of the nation. For sentimental reasons, though, given the history of a country like Scotland, is it not surely all right to give the Kirk an honoured place? An honoured place, yes, but no preeminence in regard to belief or teachings. If my thesis is correct, then there should in an open society be no official belief, no worldview institution entrenched in the affairs of the State.

But what if, as in Ireland or Poland, a religious tradition is part of the distinguishing character of the nation? Well, that is something to tell in the story of the nation, the myth of identity; but it in no wise follows that the worldview in question should be given privileges of institution.

Because the individualism which flows from the field is what I have called a 'rich individualism' it does not really need much or any substance. Its body is above all procedural. It is methodological in stance: it asks us to recognize a certain epistemology, to use empathy in understanding others, to be tolerant. In this way it can make room for entertaining a rich variety of beliefs and practices; but it does not need to affirm any one worldview. So if it contains a worldview theme it is one of attitude rather than content.

The attitude of being openminded, empathetic and tolerant is not by itself enough to govern one's own life. One needs such attitudes in a liberal democracy; but as for the particular directions of one's own existence there is need for choice, and this involves choosing a substantive worldview. But the nation does not need a single worldview.

One of the reasons for this is that the nation is not after all the community of ultimate concern. Or it ought not to be. It only has provisional status. For the individualist should if possible be free to choose her nation too. It is true that we are born as Americans or Italians or British people. But one of the best things about human civilization at its best is the possibility of emigration. Now there are constraints upon it, very severe ones in certain cases. The use of that horrid instrument, the visa, is growing in some of the traditional immigrant countries, such as Australia. But it was a nice thing in the days when *cuius regio* was formulated that the dissenting citizen was free to leave, and mostly free to arrive. Despite the growth of the resources and demands of the modern State there is still some freedom to move. One of the great symbolic powers of America is that it is the land where virtually anyone could emigrate to: it was the great alternative to southern Poland or Sweden or Kampuchea. But in so far as it is a country based upon a constitution and upon the rights of the citizen, it sets a higher law above that of national feeling. It symbolizes, for all its patriotism, the transcendence of older ethnic and religious nationhoods. It symbolizes the fact that the nation is in the last resort not ultimate: it is not the very last resort.

If there is a society of ultimate concern it should be humanity as a whole. We are now arranged in nations across the earth, but our primary loyalty ought to be humanity as a whole. Nations are ways of giving people modernity and a sense of identity: but not, if I am right, ultimate identity.

This implies, by the way, that education should prepare the young of Scotland, California or Chad in the meaning of belonging to the whole of humanity. Here Religious Studies has a vital contribution to make in telling something of the story of the world's values. One of the effects of crosscultural study is the thought that there are fine things to discover in all cultural traditions.

One of the major political problems which emerges from these wideranging concerns is the tension between individualism and liberty on the one hand and economic welfare on the other. This happens as a result of the configuration of our world at the end of the colonial epoch. It is a reasonable hypothesis that some measure of capitalism is necessary for a pluralistic society. There are no cases of completely non-capitalist societies in which individual freedom exists. This of course is not to say that capitalism always *favours* freedom. Far from it: it often favours the Pinochets of this world. Repressive and corrupt dictatorship is often the choice of big companies. In its dealings with the people of the South, capitalism has often gone into alliance with varying forms of colonial exploitation. So there is often conflict between capitalism and the desires of the poor for a better life and for newly found national independence. So although capitalism in some degree may be so far as we can see a necessary ingredient in a pluralistic society, it is also often in conflict with desires for collective liberty, and may even be in conflict with ideals of political pluralism. It is not unreasonable for people in the Third

World sometimes to think that the solution to their problems may lie in socialism, a kind of anti-capitalism. Your enemy's enemy may be your friend.

Moreover, the pluralism I advocate may not be at first a primary aim of anticolonial liberators: solidarity and nation-building may be thought to be a good deal more important.

In this way, anticolonial movements shift in a variety of directions. But the world market is dominated by the North. The prices of commodities are fixed in London and New York, Chicago and Hong Kong. What can the poorer countries do?

The state of the world is reminiscent of the times when Roosevelt came to power. There are many, many poor in the world; but now we are not just dealing with the economic problems of a single, albeit large society, the United States, but with the whole world, as a single complex market-place. As Brandt and Heath recognized in their commission which produced *North–South*,[4] a kind of Neo-Keynesian solution is now needed on a world scale. More resources need to be put into the South, so that it can buy the products of the North. We need a new way to a cycle of prosperity, and that in turn involves sarifices which will yet be in the long term interests of the North. The programme envisaged is a kind of social–democratic one, on a global scale; and it may be that the function of governments is to act like unions on behalf of their citizens to exert pressures on the Northern multinational corporations. To all this a Marxian analysis is not particularly relevant. Human experience with welfare socialism, that is social–democratic, forms of economy is good; but with absolute socialism it is on the whole bad. And that is encouraging – for it augurs reasonably for relative freedom in the emerging countries, when they recognize the productivity of freedom.

But times are not propitious in other directions for individual freedom: computers create too much information and misinformation about people; we are currently in a conservative mood politically in many of the Northern democracies, and not all that active in maintaining a pluralist perspective; new technologies of brain control may emerge from neurophysiological research. So we need to be on our guard. And here the religions themselves can make a special contribution. For in so far as they speak with two voices, one earthly and the other heavenly, they may have a more potent direction from which a critique of secular values can be made.

That is, given that now there has been a crumbling of authority, it does not mean that religion has become irrelevant. On the contrary that 'other shore' to which religion points and of which it speaks is the place from which to criticize this world. The task of religious doctrine is now one of criticism, not dogmatism. The visions which the faiths inspire are alternative pictures of this world, and modes of rescuing individual dignity from the toils of a technocratic civilization. So the aim of the study of religion – to understand the other – may be supplemented by drawing on those very resources which religion reveals, in order to criticize the shortcomings and oppressions of this world. This is where what I have called a rich individualism scores over the restricted individualism of an older liberalism. It is liberalism plus a variety of cultures, plus the depth supplied by the resources of the trans-cendentalist religions. It is Popper, empathy and heaven!

If the liberalism I have been advocating is against establishment in education, it is also of course against it in the State. In Britain religious establishment focuses finally on the Queen. I am not so radical as to say we should do away with the Royal Family; but we could surely evolve it away from its religious connections. If there is to be a way of entrenching pluralism it could be done through a Senate in which representatives of many differing viewpoints could be included, as part of some balanced way of inducing variety. But I am not sanguine about such structural changes in British society. Maybe the best that we can do is at least to begin to *think* plurally.

This will have great effects in all of education. In history it should mean that all history should be in the context of world history. It may be countered that we have enough to do already with British and European history. But with syllabus-designers we always have enough, more than enough. To cover greater areas you need to be more selective, of course. But that is not in itself difficult. Then in literature we shall have to be comparative. One of the best experiences I had when young was being intro-duced at Glasgow Academy to Russian literature by an eccentric but gifted teacher, who had no special business introducing me to Russian literature seeing that we were doing English literature. Since then I have had my life enriched by Turgenev and Dosto-ievsky. That Mr Crosbie was an educator with a feel for the wider world, and I here pay tribute to him. So: literature should be comparative, and set in world perspective. And the teaching of

worldviews should be plural and empathetic, and only then critical. The teaching of science should be enlivened by the history
of science so that young folk may see that most scientists in the
past were wrong. Only in mathematics should we allow talk of
proof! But even here Riemann and Lobachevski should haunt the
geometers: let noone without these geometers enter the academy!
The educated young person in Britain would be already feeling
a world citizen, would be self-confidently critical in her opinions,
and tolerant of varying points of view.[5]

All this might involve a weakening of traditional loyalties: if a
Catholic, then a questioning Catholic; if a Presbyterian, a Presbyterian interested in yoga; if an atheist, an atheist with slivers
of vision of the Beyond; if patriotic then critical of national values;
if virtuous, then pluralistic in values; if committed, then freely
committed. It is an ideal difficult to achieve, but it is implied by
the logic of worldview analysis.

It might be argued that the ideal is not only difficult: it does not
appeal to political leadership. Its erosion of obedient patriotism is
not something which a government will wish to encourage. Why
should taxpayers subsidize teachings which undermine the loyalty of citizens? On this several observations are apposite.

First, in so far as the world-wide, pluralistic outlook is itself a
worldview,it is one that overlaps greatly with the ideals of liberal
democracy. Now it may be asked whether there is not an implicit
conflict between liberal democracy as a universal ideal and the
particularism of nationality. There is such a tension. But a nation's
citizenry needs more than just appeal to nationality if the continuing sacrifices demanded of it are still going to be willingly
made. In the past, often the overriding ideological justification
from intra-national altruism has been a traditional religion. In
Marxist countries it has been Marxism–Leninism. In America it
has been a blend of values including those of the Enlightenment,
as embedded in the Constitution. So the fact that I appeal to
universal values of global solidarity and critical pluralism is natural enough: there are no greater difficulties combining these ideas
with British patriotism or any other variety than in combining
(say) Christianity. In the one direction we have clashes between
national interests and universl human concerns, in the other
direction between patriotic war and the Lord's Prayer, especially
in Spanish!

There is nothing noble in putting your own national or tribal group first in policy. We are often deceived into thinking that ethnic selfishness is noble because individual people, often young men, need to make the most stupendous sacrifice, of life itself, on behalf of ethnic interests. Extra-national selfishness depends upon intra-national altruism: often our citizens are sold on the latter by appeal to universal moral principles, so that teaching Christian values can be seen to coincide with teaching intra-national altruism. What is good for the tribe is found, in this way, in the Sermon on the Mount. And in a way death for the tribe would for many be unbearable if it were not that somehow it is death for humanity. Perhaps on occasion it is – as in the fight against the Nazis. But the Nazis themselves represent a disease of nationalism, not something which attacks the root of the patriotism that Churchill mobilized to defeat Nazism. Well, if we sometimes bring in universal principles to back national identity, why not see ourselves as pioneers of world civilization, of religious and worldview pluralism, or critical freedom? If the critical international pluralism which is presupposed by the very sinews of education is a worldview theme at least, then why not adopt it as our civil religion? No doubt we can find many resources in our own history to back up this theme? Britain has not been wanting in the voices of pluralism, universal humanity and critical freedom. In brief, if now we have the watery Christianity and partial democracy which serves as the worldview underpinning our tribal identities, why not equally switch to a more robust and universal individualism? Anyone who wishes to follow Christ can still do so.

Second, critical individualism is not in the long run against the interests of the State, so long as the State is concerned with the economic welfare of the citizenry. For the individualism and pluralism which I have been advocating are themselves vital ingredients in the development of modern technological capitalism. If there is a lesson to be learned by the contemporary economic state of the world it is to be found in the vital character of open education. In some ways British education is better than that found in California, but Californian education is having more punch in the development of new forms of high technology, and the reason I believe is that the young of California are more daring, ambitious and wide ranging in their interests. It is a heady brew of pluralistic living, with possibilities of exploiting new ideas. So we have in California a simultaneous revolution in ideas and living. It is not a coincidence that there are so many new lifestyles in California: the culture breeds both experimentation in living and in thinking. So it actually helps the State of California to broaden and deepen its tax base, this adventurous quality. For all its profoundly civilized merits, British education tends more towards conformism, of doing things thus because tradition tells us that things are indeed done thus. And because innovation is not widely spread the true inventions of Britain are not rapidly exploited, or their patents are sold in America and maybe in Japan. In brief, an open education may in fact be seen by rulers as in conformity with the interests of the State.

Third, the internationalist aspect of education fits with the growing facts of global life. We are increasingly in the world dominated by the transnationals, and governments themselves often function as agents and facilitators of the transnational companies. This being so, knowledge of the wider world is often a great advantage. If American education is weak in this respect, it is so far compensated for by two things – one is the relative, though by no means absolute, dominance of American-based transnationals; and the other is the fact that America contains still enough people who have come from anywhere you care to mention to provide a pool of talent and knowledge related to that region of the world. Even so, some educators in the United States are beginning to worry about the parochialism of Americn education, and it is indeed a factor in various errors and misjudgments in US political and commercial policy in the wider world.

So an open internationalist education is not without its attractions to our rulers. It represents a worldview-theme that can be built into our sense of national identity. But to do it effectively we need to drop the cant of establishment, the pretence that ours is a 'Christian country', the notion that we have some monopoly of common-sense and rationality. We need to defy the implicit claims both of theology and philosophy. It is perhaps a propitious time to cast off some of our traditional ways of thinking about education, for the crisis which afflicts so much of higher education in Britain and elsewhere means that we need new thinking to reshape our goals with the relatively limited resources we now have and to begin a push for recognition of the benefits both of economics and of the spirit that might arise from new freedoms.

But the revolution which we need, overthrowing the mental

controls which States tend to impose upon citizens, cannot simply
be a revolution in one country. There is a final set of thoughts
which the vision of openness generates and which maybe I can
set briefly before you.

The revolution towards individualism and a tolerant openness
does ultimately need to be universal in scope. Ultimately it is not
much good if it is only citizens of the northern democracies who
have equal rights, protection against the State and a reasonable
standard of living. If the citizens of Cuba, Angola, Ethiopia, Chile,
Peru, Algeria, Romania and so on are neither free nor prosperous,
how can the free people of the North be happy? The logic of open
education and a plural regard for others is that all human beings
are our community. Patriotism erodes, save as the principle that
we have a set of nations like families, nurturers of identity, but
not having ultimate calls upon citizens. Yet there is so much in
today's world which builds in the concept of the sovereignty of
nation-States. It is assumed that though cruelties occur in this
country or that the governments in question have at least a prima
facie right to inflict them. Only in a few cases of flagrant villainy
would others think of interfering. The case of Kampuchea is
chilling. For policy reasons certain major states, notably the US,
Britain and China, still recognize the Khmer Rouge succession
against the Vietnamese-imposed regime. The latter is no paragon
of virtue, but the former was relatively the most homicidal regime
in the bloody history of the Twentieth Century.

It therefore seems reasonable for us to ask to whom is our
ultimate allegiance? Which is our community of ultimate concern?
For many, it remains the nation-State. Your ultimate duty is to
your own ethnie. By 'ultimate' duty I mean: Who would you die
for? To whom do you assign the power of life and death? It is for
most people no longer the family or the clan.

There is as yet no world Government. Nevertheless, it is the
teaching of many great religions, and it is in the logic of the
present enquiry, that the ultimate community is or ought to be
the human race. If we still have special bonds to our ethnic or
national group, this is in itself no harm, provided a kind of
utilitarianism prevails: we do not want everyone to be taking in
each other's washing, and the division of the earth's surface
among nations has a convenience to it that we should go along
with. It is better for me to police my region and for Swedes to
police theirs. But ultimately we are to be considered human

beings. Basically we are persons, and secondarily Italians, Catholics and what have you.

For this reason, freedom of migration itself becomes a very important matter: it means that you are not tied down to being Soviet or American or British but can have the choice of lives and of nationalities. But the complex events of the half-century or more since the Nazis seized power in Europe mean that we are now perhaps sated with migrants and refugees. Maybe so: but the principle remains vital.

Fortunately the symbolisms of our world are making it easier for us to conceive of and indeed feel ourselves as part of a universal human group. Thus in the *Los Angeles Times* of 4 February 1985 we read:

> Sophisticated remote sensing devices in space, coupled with super computers that can process staggering amounts of information, have made it possible for scientists to plan a project that is so ambitious and complex that it would have been out of reach just a few years ago.
>
> The technology should be available within the next few years to permit scientists from a wide range of disciplines to study the Earth as a single ecosystem, increasing the odds that the planet will continue to support life in the future.

The item went on to describe a meeting in Pasadena lately to plan an international and interdisciplinary 'mission to planet Earth' – a project for answering questions about the earth as a total life-support system. Already such a project trails a large number of symbolic values. Already those pictures of the earth from half way to the moon give us a symbolic feel for such transnational plans, and make being a Russian or a Scot or a Ghanaian less significant. No longer is the human habitat something indefinite 'the wide, wide world': it is a beautiful green, blue and white ball, small against the infinite spaces which once frightened Pascal.

All this reinforces the need for education to help with the process of generating a sense of historical identity. We need, as I have repeated more than once, to teach world history, and to emphasize the multiplicity of cultural pasts to which this planet is heir.

Out of all this a new world culture is beginning to emerge. We shall not escape backlashes as the acids of individualism erose some aspects of existing cultures. We shall all have to live in mingled ways with mingled worldview themes, and because this is uneasy for many people there will be small nationalisms and fervid demands for ethnic independence. The bomb and the bullet will still express the hardness of fanaticism, and will still serve those who recognize that the new pluralism does indeed soften older identities at the edges.

A federalism of tolerance gives more scope for difference than any of the homegenies: if ours represents a worldview-theme, it at least allows individuals and groups great freedoms to choose the worldviews that they will live by. Most people will get 80 per cent of what they might wish for, and that is a great advance on some getting everything and others virtually nothing. For power too has to be distributed among individuals and groups. Within the vast mosaic of human experiments in living there may be places where as yet individuals have little freedom. But with good fortune the time will come when indeed we can choose how to live. Those countries such as America and Britain which turn towards an open pluralism can pride themselves on being at the forefront of a movement when the Earth will be our only country, and diversity our watchword.

3

The Intellectual Implications of Religious Studies

In turning now to the intellectual implications of the study of religion I am not leaving the subject of the way things should be taught in schools as well as universities. Let me repeat that there is no call to make any sharp divide between what goes on earlier and what goes on later in education. Unless we are clear about the so-called higher things, how can we be clear about the lower? Recent work on religious education in the primary school context has been hampered by lack of agreement on a theory of myth: for such a theory will influence how we use stories with children. So in looking to the wider intellectual implications of the study of religion we are involved in a practical as well as a theoretical survey. At the same time we shall be taking up some themes already touched on earlier.

The first lesson which is important, I think, for the wider world is a repudiation of what may be called 'methodological rationalism', that is the attitude that one may understand the way other cultures work partly in terms of a universal model of rationality: roughly the Macintyre rather than the Winch position in that famous debate. The fact is of course that humans are partly rational beings, and I do not deny that similar forms of reasoning may occur in differing cultures. But we cannot take some model of what counts as a contradictory utterance as a norm of what can or cannot be believed. For actual contradictions are embedded in contexts: and seeming contradictions likewise. The latter are not to be judged externally, but internally. From the point of view of their effects on human behaviour what counts is whether they are seen as contradictions. Thus the Copenhagen School, by

inventing the concept of complementarity, eased a sense of possible contradiction, and were able to carry on reasonably comfort-
ably. It is important to practise *epoche* regarding the *logic* of other
cultures and other groups, since the logic that has effect is largely
applied logic, and application lets in the influences of a worldview.

The question is important, owing to the prevalence of methodological rationalism in Western philosophy at the present time.
A particular worldview, namely scientific humanism, has become
dominant, despite the softenings of position implied by the more
socially and historically oriented interpreters of the tradition, such
as Richard Rorty and Kuhn, Feyerabend and Putnam[1] and other
of the softer philosophers of science. Philosophy in the modern
English-speaking tradition is in the business of trying to refine
and expound a worldview: and at the same time it has become
highly professionalized, seeing rigour in dialectical skills, analytic
delicacy and a degree of ideological conformism. This was
especially marked in the period from the early fifties to the mid-
1970s. More pluralism is evident today, with increased interest
among English-speaking philosophers in such Continental European thinkers as Heidegger and Habermas. But even that pluralism is Eurocentric, and suggests alternative species of worldview
to the older analytic humanism. There has not been much broad-
ening out to other non-European worldviews.

Such analytic humanism has been reinforced by the turn
towards speculative ethics: Rawls, for instance, provides a much-
debated model of justice in a worldview-vacuum. That is, there
is an assumption that ethics is indeed autonomous. Some of the
assumptions of recent approaches to ethics and applied ethics
are, it is true, challenged by Macintyre's *After Virtue*[2]: but from
an essentially European perspective.

It is not for me to deny that scientific humanism is the right
worldview: but there are, as we have already seen, many issues
arising about how we know whether a worldview is true and
another false. But do we feel justified in institutionalizing it in
departments of philosophy? This is often the fact. This is brought
out by the way in which the philosophy of religion is often
treated. It is regarded as rather peripheral in philosophy departments, though it has to be taught because of student interest. The
best-regarded tend to be those who like Plantinga, Swinburne
and D. Z. Phillips[3] play in the technical and ideological leagues

of the dominant ideology: they do subtle things, but they remain also, in religion, tied to the narrowest conceptions of Western theology. But if we expand philosophy of religion to the philosophy of worldviews, and consider it the mode in which we look at the criteria of truth as between and among worldviews, then it is obviously central to the non-technical parts of philosophy. For philosophy is, after all, traditionally and in some degree even today, considered as the love of widsom, and wisdom here has to do with which is the right or most fruitful worldview. So though philosophy has many virtues, it at the moment needs to make its position about worldviews much clearer. Its problems indeed have to do largely with this lack of explicitness and outer connections. It needs to do more than it is now doing in the sociology of knowledge, and seeing some of the symbolic roots of its worldview preferences. Worldview analysis and the exploration of criteria for evaluating worldviews become a central aspect of pluralistic philosophy, and in this way the fields of religious studies and philosophy merge.

But though this is so, in another respect they do not. For the interests of philosophers, as they have grown up in the modern Western world, are conceptual. It is a disease of the study of religion to be conceptual to the exclusion of other aspects, such as ritual and music, which are vital to the actual life of religions and worldviews. And in its own way the study of religion takes a course half way between the history of ideas and anthropology.

The empirical exploration of worldviews does, of course, have considerable conceptual implications. I think the treasure-house of alternative cultures in the world may make us alive to alternative ways of ordering our concepts. Since the Enlightenment we have come to be used to the normal character of discussion of freedom of the will, the mind–body distinction and human rights, even though many major traditions put things quite differently. There is no concept of free will in traditional China, nor is the distinction between mind and body made at all in the same way in the Indian tradition, and the idea of human rights is absent from non-European cultural traditions (other ideas perform a similar but not quite the same function of protecting individuals – e.g. the concept of *li* in the Confucian tradition). I am not saying that the notions and distinctions which we wield in the West are mistaken: but they are at least contingent, and we ought to be aware of this. Alternative cultures and other ways of ·

cutting the conceptual cake can be a stimulus to our imagination. So comparative worldview analysis can become among other things a conceptual resource to spur thinking about the fundamental categories which we need. It is especially important that we emphasize this conceptual diversity at the present time because there are dangers in the present world economy of homogenization of culture among the best-educated stratum of people, borne by jets from Tokyo and Nairobi to Delhi and Oslo in a new Westernized noosphere. There is the danger that diversity will be for peasants. One of the main claims of Religious Studies upon the intellectual world lies in the fact that in the last three or four decades particularly religionists above all (though not exclusively) have kept alive and deepened Western knowledge of Asian philosophies, such as Samkhya, Vedanta, Neo-Confucianism, Chinese syncretic religion, modern Japanese synthetic philosophies, medieval Islamic kalam and philosophy, Jewish Kabbalah, and Russian Orthodox thought, etc. It is to anthropology that we should look primarily in preserving small-scale worldviews: but it is to the interest in Eastern cultures especially, fueled by the student revolt of the late 1960s and early 1970s, that we should look in the heavy development of comparative and traditional worldview analysis. But there has been less impact from the richnesses provided so far than one might have desired, on the intellectual scene as a whole. But at least the materials are being assembled for new ways of looking at our conceptual and other categories. In brief, worldview pluralism brings into view conceptual diversities: at the least these may be stimuli for new ways of looking at the world – stimuli to the worldview-construction which is one of the tasks of philosophy, and stimuli too to creating new approaches to older problems.

If the disease sometimes of Religious Studies is over-conceptualization, at least the concern with doctrines is some counterweight to anthropological emphasis upon symbols and rituals. Actually, what is needed is a new synthesis between historical and partly-conceptual analyses of traditions and anthropological-type explorations of religion on the ground. It happens that the smaller-scale traditions are changing rapidly under the impact of global forces, both economic and religious–ideological. The traditional larger-scale religions are actually likely to prove more important for the future, and it is here that a new birth of religious anthropology is beginning to take place: I am thinking of syntheses such as those of Richard Gombrich in Sri Lanka, Stanley Tambiah in Thailand, William Christian in Spain,[4] and various developing sociological and anthropological studies of Christian Europe. At any rate, we are maybe entering a new phase in the history of ideas and of the sociology of knowledge. One area where the matter of worldview analysis could much illuminate our understanding is in the field of political science. Many new movements in the world have political vitality, and it is important to understand in particular the relations between reaffirming identity in a religious and cultural context on the one hand and political action on the other. So let me illustrate something of the effects of the modern study of religion on the analysis of our world by considering what I have elsewhere called Position Theory. Here I shall expand what I earlier talked about as Syncretistic Realism.

Position Theory[5] is the view that a religious or cultural tradition has only a number of positions to occupy, once it is under challenge from another powerful tradition. As a limiting case, a tradition may opt for a kind of obliviousness, which I shall call the Oblivion Position. One is reminded of the villages in India where not only did they not realize the British had left, but did not even know they had ever been there. But the facts of the modern world involve the injection into traditional societies of a whole slew of new cultural influences. Most traditional cultures have undergone the colonial impact of the West, which has also been the agent of the introduction of among other things modern science and technical methods. Though these in principle have no motherland, they can seem like alien forces when they arrive: but forces too that can have immense attraction, partly because of the riches that they promise, but mainly because of the prestige that plays around them. So traditional culture has to come to terms with these forces, and typically it is by a simultaneous process of inner reform and absorption from outside. Some aspects of traditional society and thinking have to be rejected. But a tradition is a rich thing, and has various phases and wide resources, which can be drawn on. The modern culture can use its powers of Resource Selectivity. Differing elements and periods of the past are moved into the forefront in the attempt to cope with the incoming forces.

The forces in question are: modern science and technological knowhow, colonial oppression but at the same time the ideals of national liberation, democracy, socialism and capitalism. The most important of these has turned out to be, first in Europe and then in the wider world, nationalism. This itself has many of the properties of a religion: it has its rituals of flag, parade and battle; its myth of national history and ancestors among sages, poets, musicians; its experiences of exaltation and patriotic fervour; its ethics of self-sacrifice and good citizenship; its sacred institutions, such as the party and the army, the schools and the presidency. The aim of wars and other struggles is national independence: but since the national unit, however defined, has tended to be the unit through which people have modernized – industrialized, reorganized education for the modern epoch, and so on – the aim of national struggle has often coincided with the ideology of modernity.[6] Sometimes socialism has been adopted as a route to renewal as a protection against capitalism, which has often come in the wake of colonial domination and has been associated with humiliation and injustice. So usually what the struggling new nation may wish for is a combination of traditional values, modernity and some form of social reconstruction. The problem is in part that faced by China in the last century: can one have Confucian values and (Western) technological expertise?

All this typically implies a form of Resource Selectivity in which a tradition reaches into its past to come up with a 'modern' view of the tradition. Sometimes these new blends are looked on in Western reportage as fundamentalism, but this is not an apt or discriminating word. Sometimes a tradition attempts to reconstruct itself by going back to the foundational period. Thus Libyan Islam is a blend of such Foundationalism (even the Hadith are rejected) with modern notions of technology, capitalism and socialism. The aim is to show that such Neofoundationalism is the 'real' Islam: not the intervening more decadent forms which were among other things associated with colonial conquest. Or a tradition may go back to the Postfoundational period as crucial, as with modern Iranian Islam, with its emphasis on the early Caliphate, the Shi'i succession and the martyrdom themes of that period. Later Shi'i passivity in face of government, Greek philosophy and a whole lot of medieval and premodern Islamic themes are swept aside as the cause of present social and political discontents. This is Neopostfoundationalism. Sometimes it is apt to reach back into the classical period, as with Indian Neovedanta, from Vivekananda onwards. Such Neoclassicism also incorporates prior foundational values, of course. (Other Hindu reforming movements such as the Arya Samaj were Neofoundationalist.) One can look on the Moral Majority as a Neofoundationalist ideology, blending Biblicism and patriotism. In Sri Lanka a kind of going back to 'early Buddhism' as itself being modern and scientific forms the basis of what Heinz Bechert has called Buddhist Modernism.

But on occasion the old ideologies do not work to combine national reconstruction and modernity. The national movements of Asia have also experienced the need to reach out of their own tradition, and to lift an ideology, Marxism, from the West, as a means of restructuring society. Marxism as the 'anti-ideology' of the West, being against capitalism, liberalism and colonialism (that is, national chauvinism), could function quite well if adapted in the struggle for national liberation. Thus in China the means of reshaping independence was Maoism. By contrast Japan reached back into the mythology of the Shinto tradition to copy the Western imperial model. It was fortunate in MacArthur, who imposed on the country a new system, combining capitalism, democracy and religious pluralism.

Also in smaller scale societies there are acute problems of identity. Often such groups are not big enough or favourably placed to form the basis of separate nations. New religious movements, such as the Black African independent churches, are important new symbolic syntheses which attempt to combine Christianity, Africanness and certain structural features of the preceding Classical African religions. Similarly elsewhere in the smaller societies caught up in the vast impact of the Western conquests.

This then is a brief and rough sketch of the various positions which traditions may adopt in the search for a way of coping with the impact of colonial rule, Christian evangelism and capitalist economic changes. Such a Position Theory takes seriously the notion that worldviews are important, that traditional religions offer various possibilities of Resource Selectivity and that analysis of the blends is a fruitful way to understand some of the major political movements in today's world. It is important to recognize that the washing away of any rigid distinction between religion and secular worldview – or between religious and secular themes, such as modernity, national identity and so forth – is an intrinsic presupposition of the effective analysis of worldviews. If the religionist has any advantage as analyst, it is just that there are merits in moving from traditional to modern secular symbolisms, and from religious myths to secular ones, since it is often a property of the effective symbol or myth that it is so to speak unnoticed. It appears as 'natural' and so it can better be exposed and analysed beginning from the area where there is a more explicit and traditional search for myth and symbol.

We may apply the insights of worldview analysis to the study of history. It is an interesting fact that in most countries the education system lays a lot of emphasis upon teaching the young history. This is a modern phenomenon. The stories of traditional societies were often rather different in style: the ancestors came out of a hole in the ground; or were ruled over by a fertile and wonder-working queen; or were suckled by a wolf; or whatever. The style once was mythological; but in modern times the style has to be factual, realistic, solidly so far as possible established in documents and stones. Yet the function of the stories may in fact be very much the same: primarily they are told in order to give us a sense of identity. Only now *we* are only in part identified by descent. The genealogy of ancestors is not important, even if it is nice from time to time to uncover particular roots. Our descent is traced by cultural means: we are born into a particular stream of history. The stories told as history tell us which stream. With that history come particular art works, music and literature. Artists are important figures in our cultural ancestry. But there are tensions between history as identity-giving myth and the critical realism demanded by modern scientific methods as used to establish what the facts were. This tension is most acutely expressed in the debates surrounding Christian origins, where older mythic modes were blended with historical claims, and where today's scholars have become increasingly uncertain about the realism of the original Gospel claims. Since in modern times the nation has become identified with territory, the way a story is presented may be bound up closely with the territorial claims of the modern State: thus the stories told in Argentine and British schools were rather different in relation to the Malvinas. The history of Israel is told in a special way to justify modern occupation of the territory of the State.

The foregoing discussion indicates ways in which an appreciation of the symbolic force of aspects of everyday existence is brought to the forefront of consciousness as a result of the study of religion. It is a kind of anthropological perspective, but anthropology applied as much to us as to them, and applied in the contexts of modernity. It is an attitude, moreover, which is suspicious of rationalism as an ingredient in the explanation of human affairs. Of course the fact that myth and symbolism may be important in understanding the grip of certain ideas has upon us in no way entails that we have ourselves to think as mythically as possible. It may be that a rationalistic outlook is central to the right worldview, and that we should rise above the level of symbolic thinking which so much determines the directions of human history and the viability of the positions to which traditions are open.

The study of religion, however, is likely to make us interested in the forces which have animated the great religious figures of the past and present, for instance, the kinds of religious experience which have helped to nourish religion and give life to the more formalized aspects of traditions. For instance, it is not unreasonable to take seriously the quest for mystical experience that has been so vital a feature of virtually all the great religions, and is summed up in the varieties of yoga and meditation coming out of the South Asian tradition. It is not necessary, to appreciate such experiences, to assume the existence of God, even if most of the traditions which have helped to stimulate and express mystical experience have had some concept of the Transcendent. We are, it seems to me, only at the beginning of the investigation of mysticism, and though some progress has been made since the days of William James, there is a long way to go before we have any certainties about the nature of the varieties of religious experience. The topic is of wide intellectual interest, it seems to me, not only because religious experience remains one of the modes under which we experience the world, but also because without a crosscultural approach we have no means of estimating the force of projectionist theories of religion.

It is obvious that such theories lie at the heart of certain modern theories of human nature, such as those of Marx or Freud. But the original basis of them was from one phase of Western culture. The more complex reality revealed by the history of religions would, to say the least, cause radical changes in the shape of projectionist accounts. And it may be that it is too soon in any event to come to conclusions of this kind in so tricky and variegated a context.

This leads to a more general reflection about the role of the crosscultural study of religion and worldviews in today's intellectual world. The field is the most vital one in reminding people in the West of the genuine diversity of the world. It reminds people of the facts and values of great civilizations other than our own, and of the religious matrices which gave birth to them. It does so more easily than other social scientists: than sociology which tends to be home-based; and than anthropology which tends to draw its material from the weaker societies which can thus too easily be 'looked down upon' from the standpoint of the modern Westerner. I remember once my wife (who is Italian) and I were attending a show of local Chumash Indian paintings in Southern California. She was asked what she thought of them. She answered, alas with deadly truth: 'When they were doing those rock paintings, *we* were doing the Sistine Chapel.' Well, of course, it was a matter of the scale of economic and cultural organization. But had my wife been Japanese or Chinese or Indian or Iranian she could have said something similar. It is not a matter of East and West or North and South, but of scale. And the comparative study of religion can remind us of rivals to the European–American achievement. And this by the way is not to say that the smaller-scale societies have nothing to offer: it is just that anthropology in presenting them is presenting societies which can still secretly or overtly attract some kind of racist superiority syndrome. But put all non-Western cultures together and we have some powerful antidotes to such a syndrome. Of course in the long run the 'Anything you can do I can do better, or earlier, or whatever' sentiment is childish. But it is useful as a first move to remind Westerners of the great depth of alternative traditions, and this will help to create more of a crosscultural and pluralistic mentality.

The study of worldviews as alternative itself may moderate the trivialization of culture which is one trend in multicultural adjustment. It is what may be called the 'folklorization' of cultures. Certain aspects of a total culture are selected out as relatively harmless and, more positively, colourful: and then the culture is represented by and identified with these features – such as traditional dress, arts, dance, music, cooking and so on. Scottishness becomes: kilt, bagpipes, haggis; Chineseness is dragons, chopsticks and wok; Indianness is natya, curry and the sari. The biting edge of difference is left out, for that is found along the contours of the different worldviews found in the cultures. It is a common ploy, such folklorization, in the polite suppression of pluralism. With the move goes the cultivation perhaps of the traditional language. Thus the Soviet Union is generous in its outlays on regional languages and folklore, but yet within a rigidly imposed single worldview which itself involves the suppression of values inherited with the cultural traditions, such as Islam in Soviet Central Asia, and nationalist sentiment in Georgia, and so on. Since religions are often hot and difficult political issues, there is widespread omission of this dimension of cultural existence.

This is partly a consequence of the ghettoization of religion – its privatization – in Western countries. But it is also a consequence of imperial rationalism: that is the assumption of a particular worldview as commanding not just our heights but also the world's heights. And this is part of that lack of pluralism to which the study of religion and religions is one of the prime antidotes. This is where I would again lay strong emphasis upon the idea of worldview analysis. The division between religion and secular ideologies allows the latter to make a move like that of Karl Barth and Hendrik Kraemer,[7] the Dutch theologian who applied ideas of dialectical theology to the problems of the mission field in his influential *The Christian Message in a Non-Christian World* of 1938. The Christian move was to say that all religions as such are man-made. The Christian religion is likewise so, save that it is a response to the revelation in Christ (which is an event or series of events emanating from God). It reflects the influence of revelation. But that is a secondary matter: the important thing is that the Christian relates to transcendental revelation: all religions are essentially human constructions and do not play in the same league. The Christian therefore has no problem of other religions. I do not want to go into the varied objections to this position, beyond pointing out that the Hindu or Buddhist could reverse the argument. Everything is humanly made except the Dharma, Emptiness or whatever. The secular-ideological position is not dissimilar. All religions are projections. But 'our' position (Marxism, humanism, etc.) is not. The division between religion and secular view is an invitation not to relativize one's own secular position.

The demands of self-analysis, however, in the study of religion open up some interesting questions, for instance in relation to Habermas' drive to become somehow 'ideology-free'. It is of course interesting that the Marxist tradition has involved itself greatly with the issues arising from the theory of false consciousness which lead to a critique of all possible ideologies including Marxism itself. One is reminded of the predicament of those who follow Nagarjuna, another variety of critical philosophy. The teachings of the Buddha himself fall under the hammer of dialectic. The only reason for following the Buddha is that he invented the dialectic! Well, Marxist self-criticism may likewise subvert Marxism: but ironically Marxisms have been among the most effective worldviews in recent times in creating leverage upon the historical process.

One can of course use the study of worldviews to reinforce relativism and so induce scepticism. Why adopt any worldview? Let us just act so to speak in the midst of things. But I would only add that the exploration of forms of religious experience may become more, not less, important: for with no worldviews to underpin and with no apologetics and criticism to worry about the spiritual experience of the world and of other persons might become the more available, and provide a path of happiness and 'insight' not otherwise available. Perhaps this is what Nagarjuna was driving at.

If we turn from the varied conceptual frameworks, the various sets of doctrines which we find in the world at large, to the myths, it is clear that in the contemporary globe we need to take with great seriousness the project of world history, and the comparative study of civilizations. Though Toynbee has attracted, and still does to a great extent, criticism and even contempt among nitty-gritty historians, his general scheme was along the right lines.[8] He saw that religions are the overarching and formative matrices of civilizations. No doubt his theory of how civilizations arise and decline was not all that impressive: but it represents, as does the magisterial work of Max Weber, an early attempt at world history as an explanatory system. Time will show more and more crosscultural studies, for the simple reason that you cannot get a society into a laboratory, and comparative work is the next best thing, from the angle of the testing process. So we should not either treat Weber as guru or Toynbee as fool (tendencies not unobserved in recent times among intellectuals). Both are early and defective workers in the field of crosscultural comparison and world-historical interpretation. Another more recent approach is that of 'globology', now developed primarily in the United States

and using mostly sociological and economic tools, being somewhat Marxian in orientation, as it happens. This again could make
use of religious and worldview Position Theory in explaining the
dynamics of today's world.

In all this it might be replied that what I claim to be a virtue
in Religious Studies, its capacity to detribalize Westerners, can
as well or better be achieved by the study in depth of any
one of the non-Western traditions – by immersing ourselves in
Chinese, or South Asian, or African studies, and so on. I do not
deny the reply, except to say that whereas crosscultural endeavour
is intrinsic to Religious Studies, religious or worldview analysis
is not always given much prominence in non-European studies.
Sometimes scholars bring over a thin rationalism into their
approach to other cultural traditions. For what is the norm in
Western Studies can easily transfer to Orientalism or Southern
Studies. But in principle of course it is fine to immerse oneself
in Oriental, African, Pacific or other studies. But here we meet
with a phenomenon which is a problem. These areas of intellectual endeavour are still regarded as a bit odd by the mainstream
intellectual in Western universities. Many universities have no
Chinese or Indian studies. In some it is the Religious Studies
programme which sustains such non-European studies as there
are. Fortunately, in the States the increasing pluralism of the
ethnic mix often forces university administrations to take minority
cultures seriously, and in some degree similar forces are more
slowly at work in Europe and Australia.

I earlier remarked on how the very procedures of crosscultural
study of religion force upon us a kind of self-analysis. This should
be so both collectively and individually. In many ways it is in
the understanding of our own culture that the greatest fruits of
the study of religion will emerge. It is the use of religious studies
methods which will revolutionize the study of our 'home' religion.
It is through such modes that we can best understand Christianity
and Judaism. Let me illustrate this, because it needs more spelling
out than I have so far been able to accomplish here.

First, let us note that the tendency in our cultures as in others
is to treat 'our' tradition normatively, either explicitly or secretly.
I have already touched briefly on this matter, in relation to the
problem of Church and State. There are severe intellectual pen-
alties of the normative or crypto-normative approach to studying
religion. I should say before I catalogue these disadvantages that

some of my best friends are traditionalist Christian theologians, and often their work transcends in historical quality a great deal that is done in the comparative study of religions. I am not in criticizing the categories used impugning either their characters or their expertise: merely I say that their views of the subject have been shaped by a somewhat unfortunate past. Their ancestry is by Established Church out of Classicism, and this should make them of high birth.

The first penalty of the concessional kind of approach is that Christianity is not treated in its full sociological and historical richness. We still tend to write history according to the victors. Very often the subject of the history of Christianity is described as Church History. Christian origins are described as New Testament Studies. Early Christianity is referred to as Patristics. What is the Church but a normatively described mainstream Christianity? There is not a single major part or denomination of the Christian heritage that has not been denounced by some other as being heretical or schismatic. The trend goes on today. The former archbishop of Canterbury described the Moonies as not being Christian, though they want to call themselves Christian. How long will the ban last? Will they eventually become respectable? But history does not deal with respectability: but only with perceptions of respectability. It is better to have a positivistic definition of Christianity. It is a great cloud of movements. Would not the Arians and Donatists and even perhaps the Albigensians now be allowed to join the World Council of Churches, if the Kimbanguists can? Any positive history of Christianity will be a history of all movements flowing from the streams that began at the time of Jesus. And the same applies in the study of scriptures, even not canonical. It is true that modern scholarship has taken Nag Hammadi on board and a whole lot else. Maybe, as James Robinson has argued, early Christianity was nearer the Gnostics, or some of them, than we now think. And, in regard to Patristics, who have come to be counted as Fathers?

Why are the Fathers important? Largely because they are normative for many Anglicans and Orthodox Christians. But the division of history according to normative criteria has had some strange side effects. Thus you can go to one or two Canadian universities where there is intensive study of the Bible but nothing on Canadian Christianities; you could until lately be hard put to find decent work on modern Irish Christianities; until

lately there was little know about Eastern Christianities, such as
the history of Indian Christianity. Admittedly things are changing, but there is still a skew in investment of scholarly resources:
for in my view all periods of a religious tradition are as history
equally important.

But the cryptonormative heritage has some other and in a way
more serious consequences. It is that Christianity is rarely treated
in a fully dimensional way. That is, much of the work deals with
doctrines and sacred narratives, that is with the doctrinal and
mythic dimensions, but not so systematically with the other
dimensions – ethics, experience, ritual, institutions and material
expression (art, architecture, etc.). The main thrust of academic
teaching has been with the history of doctrines and to some
degree the history of Biblical interpretation. There has not been
the same concern with the history of what may be called Christian
spirituality, though things are changing now, partly under the
impact of the comparative study of religion. Often though when
these areas are studied they are explored in too 'applied' and
normative a way: spirituality or the experiential dimension is
through the 'good' examples: Rhineland mystics, rather than
flagellants; the experience of Augustine's conversion but not that
of the born again conservative. The study of ritual is often bound
up with applied liturgiology: how to reform Christian worship.
So we do not have as riched or fleshed-out a view of Christianities
as we might have. Given that traditional Christian teaching was
meant to prepare Christian priests and ministers in the truth and
the pastoral translation of that truth into practice, why should
traditional teaching not be normative and applied? Well, I have
partly dealt with that under the head of the political implications
of the pluralistic study of religion. But of course often courses
which are designed to be normative and practical are unpractical.
Students live in the 20th Century and not the 2nd or 17th, so how
are they to interpret Bible and Reform? This is partly why in the
last twenty years there has been a great development of interest
and work in 19th and 20th century religious and atheistic thought,
to begin to provide a thinking bridge from the then to the now.
But the study of Christianities on the ground is chiefly reserved
for sociologists of religion and those involved in the study of
'implicit' religion. The tendency of our theological schools, however much they may include the study of non-Christian religions
(itself an interesting category) and however much they may have

a more plural and ecumenical view of Christianity, is still over-whelmingly cerebral. After all the very word 'theology' is itself cerebral.

Incidentally, most of those who study religion and many of those enrolled in divinity schools are of course not going to be priests or ministers. They are going to teach and go into all those other professions which typically the humanities and social science graduates find themselves in. And in so far as they get involved with the questions of the young, in schools, they need a dimensional approach. The young, rightly, see the actual behaviour of religious people as relevant as what the texts and pontiffs say.

This dimensional approach gives us also, as I have already argued, an insight into secular ideologies as well. So part of the study of our home culture must be into the actual ideas and syncretisms which exist in our midst. Self-analysis thus becomes collective. We need insight not just, though, into ideas but into the various rituals which sustain our collective life. We can often see the actual nature of our life through the comparative method. We knows aught of England, or Scotland, who only England, or Scotland, knows?

Position Theory can help too to illuminate issues in the relation between religion and science. There are ways in which science as an establishment comes to take on an autonomous character not unlike an institutionalized religion. Of course, it is not strictly a religion, or even an ideology, but it nevertheless does create some sets of ideas and practices which mean that it plays partly in the same league as religions and ideologies. For instance, it can create methodological doctrines, of which probably the most potent at the moment is the philosophy of Karl Popper, which also serves as indeed a political ideology. His endorsement of the processes of open criticism has profound implications also for academic life. There is also a myth of the rise of science, which has to do in part with the conflicts of new scientific ideas and the traditional ideology of the Church, as with Galileo and Darwinism. The Enlightenment is seen as the main watershed of human history, for it brought together tendencies which could be modelled into a scientific and humanistic outlook. There is an ethic implicit in science, because the pursuit of truth according to certain methods is given high value, and contrasted with irrational acceptances of previous authority. There is a kind of priesthood: the learned societies, the range of those admitted officially into the ranks of scientists. They are often spokespersons, speaking authoritatively about the latest discoveries which might be more interesting to the mass of people. And it incorporates a series of powerful and overlapping institutions.

In some respects the situation is akin to that of Buddhism. The teachings and goal of the Buddha are not attractive or intelligible to ordinary people. So he makes use of parables and ritual and other devices to make the teachings accessible and inspiring. Likewise, science is in its inner nature neutral and a hard slog. But outside it takes on a glamour which arises in part from its wondrous applications. At the interface between the laboratory and the public a glow develops.

And out of the meeting of scientific tradition and the various worldviews varied positions come to be worked out. At the interface between science and atheism there arises scientific humanism. It has many attractions. The myth of the conflict of science and religion has some truth, because religions tend to project ancient teachings which themselves incorporate obsolete cosmologies. On the other hand, in reacting against religion, scientific humanism tends to forget about a profound and exciting range of human experiences, which remain part of the human heritage and are one reason why religion does not die out, even if, according to the scientific humanist, in a rational world it ought to. Then traditional Christianity and Judaism meet with the scientific culture, and both divide in various comparable ways. One way was pioneered by Protestantism in Germany and elsewhere: combine Christian values and science. This came to be known as 'liberal Protestantism' and has its analogue in Reform Judaism. There was in both traditions a fundamentalist (or Neofoundationalist) backlash, with varieties of resource selectivity. Sometimes this also involved selecting some parts of science and not others, notably Evolutionary Theory. In some ways it is in the philosophy of religion that the theoretical issues are being addressed: whether, for instance, you can add on a Transcendent to the cosmology of modern science. At the same time the philosophy of science is undergoing a rather anarchistic phase: with such disagreement about method, the frontiers of science themselves fade. Scientism becomes a kind of rationalism, and we have already discussed that.

I would like to end on a personal note. Though I do not think that the main thrust of the study of religion should be existential, that is in helping individuals to decide on a worldview, to make a commitment, or whatever, it cannot avoid setting the scene for such a choice. Actually, as we have noted, most people make up their real values by creating a kind of collage, in which elements are drawn from different traditions, fields and experiences. But often it seems that one tradition rather than another seems to correspond to such a collage – so we can represent worldview choice as indeed a choice between recognized worldviews. It is one task of the humanities to set such a scene, where sensitive choice of values can be developed. It is obviously not just within departments of religion and philosophy that the process goes on: it goes on in history, English and comparative literature, in sociology and elsewhere. Often we can get deeper into a faith or a worldview through a novel or poetry than by more formalistic methods, even if presented dimensionally. For literature can cut through surfaces: and the trouble with worldviews, whether religious or secular, is that they are unnervingly both profound and silly, both inspiring and bad. Let me try to indicate this mixed character, as I see it. Ultimately the educator who is concerned to make this world a better place so far as she can needs to give some encouragement to the more profound and inspiring aspects of human worldviews.

There is scarcely anything more profound than some of the sayings of Jesus. That these ethical and spiritual injunctions inspired the early church there is no doubt. They can still move us. But at the same time we have Christians trivially backing short term political aims by quoting the Bible, we have superficial discussions of whether bishops should believe in the bodily resurrection of Jesus, treated in the most literal and foolish manner on both sides, and we have shaky deductions from the tradition of solemn pronouncements about condoms and other contraceptives.

There can be little finer in the literature of the world than the moral analyses and injunctions of the Buddhist texts. But you can find in Sri Lanka Sinhala Buddhist nationalists who quote Buddhism to justify the political domination of the Tamils by the Sinhalese. I got into trouble for suggestions that statues of Christ and Shiva should be erected near the huge Buddha statue which looks across the lake which surrounds the beautiful new Parliament building at Sri Jayawardenepura in Sri Lanka last summer. Otherwise nice and sensible people were so bitten by the emotions generated by the present troubles in Sri Lanka that they could not stand back a little and see that you can be both a pluralist and a Buddhist. They were in the grip of feelings the Buddha would doubtless have condemned. If Jesus, likewise, had known the troubles the interpretations of his life would have caused he might have retreated to Bethany from Gethsemane, and eventually gone off fishing with his fellow-disciples.

We need, then, to deepen people's attitudes – to see the negative and mysterious theology as well as the affirmative, to see the depths of strangeness in science as well as its superficial applications, to grow through literature and living into deeper personal understandings, to voyage into religious experience even when espousing rationality, to read the sages of the world as well as the iconoclasts.

Ultimately our path lies beside the Buddha and Karl Popper. We have to seek profundity and criticism, a fresh experience of the world and a worry about all authorities. We must learn from the wise and be sceptical about gurus. Religious Studies, both at school and at university, has an essential role to play in this process of voyaging through this strange, strange world.

Part II
The Western World and Global Change

4

Christianity and Nationalism

In this chapter I wish to propound a theory, and then to comment on how that theory affects Christian judgments about nationalism. The first half is analytic; the second part is evaluative. The theory itself arises from one kind of history-of-religions approach to the phenomenon of the nation and the nation-State. It has, I believe, important implications for Christian thought – and for that matter for that of other religions and traditions.

First, then, the theory.

I

It is a not uncommon observation that modern nationalism functions like a religion. One way to present this point is to look at the various dimensions of religion and see how they are embodied in the modern way that nations embody themselves. I use the word 'modern' advisedly, since the nation-State and much of what goes with it are products of rather recent human history. It is convenient to see the French Revolution as a starting point for this observation, for it created or helped to create some typical features of modern nationhood.

First, the Revolution was a decisive blow against older, feudal patterns of institution and thinking. It substituted for the king the notion of the people as the ultimate source of authority. It created more effective centralized institutions, and it began the process of normalizing the mass citizen army, which reached its apogee in the enormous conscript forces of the two world wars. It also placed in power the middle classes, and helped pave the way for a post-Enlightenment ideology in which liberalism and patriotism combined. It set the scene thereby for a rationality in government which could assist the development of capitalist insitutions. Later some of these ideals could take a socialist turn.

The spread of nationalism was often by contagious reaction, and sometimes by contagion. Since the post-1789 nation State was an agent of modernity, and at the same time appealed to the concept of the people, it kindled by contagion aspirations for unity. But also the effectiveness of new nations made them powerful in empire and conquest, and conquered folk by contagious reaction wished to assert themselves against the conquerors, even if this might make them take over some of the conquerors' alien modernity in order to have the strength to fight them off.

Such modernity often involved the creation of a national language out of pre-existing dialectal traditions, in part for emotional reasons and in part because there was a need for universal primary education at least, and then secondary. Not all nations define themselves linguistically (for instance, the Irish – leaving aside the relatively ineffective attempt to revive the Gaelic – are English-speaking like the English with whom they are in a state of contagious reaction). But the linguistic mark of identity came to be the most classical one in the rise and solidification of 19th and early 20th century European nationalism, which spread so rapidly to so much of the rest of the world. Nationalism thus helped to create out of pre-existing materials a number of newly articulated languages, such as Czech, Afrikaans, standard Italian, modern Greek and so on.

It is now time to look at nationalism from the perspective of the dimensions of religion. I find it convenient to think of six dimensions, or if you wish to include hardware as an extra one, to think of seven dimensions. A religious tradition typically has the dimensions of doctrine, myth (or sacred narrative), ethics, ritual, experience and institutions: and some hardware – say, church buildings, ikons, printed literature, medals, clothing of a special sort and so forth. Naturally the amount and nature of these dimensions varies greatly: the Society of Friends and Haitian voodoo are relatively undoctrinal, Eastern Orthodoxy is strong on ritual, Hinduism's social institutionalization is very complex, Universalists lay great weight on ethics, Pentecostalism is experiential in its emphasis – and so forth. Leaving aside doctrine for the moment, the national idea is also incarnated in these dimensions. Thus:

Every nation has its modern myth, namely history, especially as taught in high schools. If a nation is short on past history, it may stretch its myth into the future – e.g. in a story of human progress. The myth includes heroes and other holy figures, such as poets, great scientists and others who give weight and substance to the nation. Every nation has its rituals – the use of the flag, singing the national anthem, sporting victories, parades, memorial days for the war dead, re-enactments of the revolution that brought the modern nation into existence, and so forth. Every nation inculcates and focuses experience – feelings of pride as evoked by the rituals, a sense of identity with one's people, and so forth. Every nation inculcates the ethics of citizenship: one must be ready to fight, to pay taxes, to be orderly, to raise families, to vote, to work hard, to help increase the GNP, and so forth. Every nation becomes incarnated, hopefully, in a State, which then employs a kind of priesthood – the teachers, especially – and creates a symbolic centre in the capital, the Presidency or Royal Family, or whatever. As for hardware, the State has its monuments, the flag, military machines, moonrockets if you are a superpower, airlines, universities, museums and so forth. Above all, it has sacred territory.

It is for such reasons that we can see nationalism as like a religion – or rather a whole lot of religions. Each people has its own religion, its own myth, ritual and so forth. And all this can be secular, in one sense of that slippery term: thus a Marxist state celebrates without any recourse to traditional religion – it has May Day, Lenin's tomb, October Revolution marchpasts, the ethics of being a good (Soviet) citizen, and so forth.

The relation of religion and State in nations can vary, for it is in effect a relation between two religions or more. And here perhaps I can diverge a moment to clarify a conceptual issue before I come to these relations. It is unfortunate that the term 'secular' is used both to mean (roughly) 'non-religious' – that is in the traditional sense of 'religious' – and, of a state, 'constitutionally pluralistic'. Thus in the second sense a secular State is one where religious credo does not constitute a legal disadvantage, where the State is, in other words, impartial about religions, provided they do not otherwise infringe the law. The debate about the secular consitution of the Republic of India has sometimes been confused by failing to distinguish these senses: for India is both highly religious and in theory religiously impartial. To avoid confusion in this paper I shall use 'religiously impartial' rather than 'secular' in my discussion of the secular State. I shall come back to this later. Meantime I shall in the other sense refer to secular worldviews or ideologies or themes to refer to non-religious systems or elements of belief and practice.

Now although nationalism is a modern ideology, a particular form of nationalism may in fact incorporate elements of traditional religion. That is, it may turn out to be not only formally religious but materially so also. The reasons are not hard to find. The survival of a people or language may have much to do with a religion, as in the case of Romania: so the prevailing myth of Romanian origins and the successful emergence of the Romanian people from a thousand years of obscurity after the Roman evacuation of the province of Dacia cannot even in a Communist context avoid ascribing to Christianity a crucial role. Thus the myth of the Romanian people is also the myth of Romanian Orthodoxy. So Romanian nationalism is already colored and fused with traditional religion. Particular religions are important definitionally in the self-consciousness of quite a number of nationalisms – Catholicism (e.g. Poland, Ireland), Reformed Protestantism (the Afrikaner people), Shi'i Islam (Iran), Buddhism (Sri Lanka Sinhala nationalism), Protestantism (Northern Ireland), State Shinto (pre-war Japan), Judaism (Israel) and so forth. But even in these cases there are complications: for instance the ideology of original Zionism was secular and modernizing, though the definition of being a Jew is either religious or at least tied to religion. The ideology of Zionism was in tension with the myth of Jewry. And in fact quite a number of nationalist movements have been ideologically secular or anticlerical, even when there is a dominant religion which enters into the mythic self-consciousness of the people: thus we have a kind of Church-State parallelism in Italy, Mexico, etc. In the 19th century the tension was often between liberal modernizers and traditional religion; in the 20th, between forms of socialism and traditional religion.

In the cases of liberal and liberal–socialist (or social-democratic) regimes the State was relatively impartial religiously. An added variety of relationship occurs when the State religion is in fact secular: that is, when the required belief-system of the citizenry is a secular worldview – such as secular Fascism or Marxism. (Perhaps only Hitler's Germany was fully totalitarian in its growing practice: both Mussolini's Italy and Franco's Spain allowed a parallelism of ideology and traditional Catholicism – there are echoes of a similar system in Ceauşescu's Romania, where, however, the regime is totalitarian but in matters of belief, so long as it does not get into politics, concessionary.)

Basically the Marxist countries are the major exponents of that old principle *cuius regio eius religio*, which under the impact of liberalism and modernity – all the post-Enlightenment pressures – has been largely abandoned in the West. Which brings me to the observation that if we were to use a more embracing term to cover both religious and secular belief and value systems, and 'worldview' is a convenient though not totally felicitous term in English, then the doctrine of the 'secular', that is the impartial, State would suffer an interesting seachange: a truly secular State would be worldviews-impartial, and so not favor any one world-view over any other. Of course in part such a State could not avoid it in so far as some traditional worldviews reject liberalism of this sort, and so do forms of hardline Marxism. But a citizen should not need to believe anything in order to possess his rights in full. It is only when his actions and intentions infringe the rights of others that the State may feel bound to intervene. But we are some distance from realizing such impartiality, partly because there remains elements of the *cuius regio* in liberal States – e.g. American civil religion, the Queen as head of the English Church, and so on. (What is needed, by the way, is a civil worldview, which might at least contain a spiritual message, namely the importance of freedom for religious and moral development and expression, and so the benefits of pluralism.)

Where anti-religious ideology is required in a State then there is a strict conflict between secular and traditional worldview, as has happened most obviously in Albania, Chinese Tibet, Pol Pot's Cambodia and elsewhere, and in a more restrained way, and at certain periods more intensely, in a number of other Marxist countries. It should be noted that in such countries also there is a secular worldview–worldview conflict too. Sometimes a regime does not worry about tradition so much, for it can be tamed, as it does about liberal–democratic ideas as an alternative worldview. So the theory and practice of democracy and liberalism are stamped upon. In the McCarthy era it was somewhat the other way round – leftwing views were oppressed.

Sometimes modernism, but not liberal pluralism, is combined with traditional religion to form a ruling worldview, as in Ghaddafi's Libya, the Ayatollah's Iran, Zia's Pakistan and Saudi Arabia,

Kuwait and elsewhere. Modernism with only limited pluralism, but an anti-religious ideological tradition, is found in modern Turkey.

These then are some of the traditional-secular patterns. Now I turn more directly to my theory.

In my exposition of the way in which nationalism can be said to be religious, because it exhibits the six or seven dimensions of religion, I left doctrine on one side. One reason is that in some cases there is not really much of it. The Scottish Nationalist for example wants independence or at least federal autonomy for Scotland, but there is no great transcendental doctrine, but rather a single principle only lying behind his demand, namely that every nation should have its own State.

But it is typically for nation-States and even more for empires (themselves typically founded on a basis of major-group nationalism) to develop a more extensive religious or secular ideology. In other words, a nation tends to add a doctrinal dimension to its patriotic self-consciousness and practice. This may specially come to the fore in times of war, because war itself demands such great sacrifices that the belief-aspect of patriotism has to be reinforced in order to justify the sufferings. A mere appeal to one's own nation's myth may be too particular and put warfare and other competitive activities on the level of collective egoism. So the myth has to be reinforced by doctrine. Even in peace this can be so, because of the need to justify austerities, taxations and the like. Apart from these pressures, it may well be of course that a nation has in some way been founded upon universal values – partly because after all the people's history may have been intertwined with Christianity or some other faith. In this case you can represent the ethics of citizenship simultaneously to be the service of God, etc. But it is sometimes the case that the modern birth of the nation has come about by Revolution, and a Revolution needs to have a set of doctrines. This is very obvious in connection with the American Revolution, the Russian Revolution and others. Typically a Revolution myth will, incidentally, bring about an OT–NT syndrome: and varying tacks are employed – the new regime as fulfilment, or as abrogation: there are 'orthodox' nationalists but also Marcionites! In Mexico, the OT was rewritten, so to speak, to give a dominant share to the pre-Columbians and their descendants, and to abrogate much of the intervening Spanish ideology.

My theory then is that there are heavy pressures, given the sacrifial character of nationalism (and the need often to give up selfish, family, clan and other interests), to graft on to it a universal doctrinal component. Your nation becomes the community of ultimate concern, to use a Tillichian expression, and needs a worldview basis to make sense of its ultimacy.

Already, however, a contradiction emerges: how can a doctrine which is *universal* not become an embarrassment in times of war and struggle? For instance, how can Christianity justify British folk fighting Argentines? Or Germans? How can Islam justify Iranians fighting against Iraqis? Or Marxism justify Chinese fighting Vietnamese? So long as disputes are largely nationalist in origin, because of the aggrandisement of contiguous national groups, etc. then ideological universalism turns out to be fraught with contradictory messages when used as a basis for national sacrifice. We have ironic and tragic pictures of bombers flattening cities in the name of Christian civilization, and cruelties projected under the aegis of a people whose message is that they are a universal light. The international aspect of Marxism becomes a justification for taking one nation's interests as paramount over another's. And so on.

Certain aspects of a universal worldview may lend themselves well to national identity and sense of power. Thus socialism in talking of 'the people' can tacitly identify the people with the nation or with the dominant group in the State. Traditional Christianity, and notably Catholicism, because of its hierarchical character, blends sometimes with authoritarian regimes – the army, for instance, is a parallel hierarchy.

But on the other hand, worldviews in being embodied often in a transnational institution – of which the most conspicuous is the Roman Catholic Church – can be in tension with nationalisms. The suspicion of the Papacy amid the Chinese Communists showed this tension, for instance.

Other tensions exist, arising in part from the universal ideologies which help to underpin the doctrines of particular nationalisms. Much to the point is the individualism of modern Western democracies. Major elements of it have to be sacrificed in wartime: free speech, consumer choice, liberty of movement, and so on. But even in peace there are tensions: the individual in contemporary life in the West begins to think of herself as a citizen of the world, and among many nations it has been relatively easy to migrate (even if the requirements of labour certification in a period of unemployment have imposed new difficulties). The Christian who takes liberal individualism seriously is likely to take the ecumenical movement seriously too: as a world Christian, then, his sense of not primarily belonging to a country but to the human race may be reinforced.

It is doubtful whether any nation can be stable over the long run unless the majority accept in principle the ruling ideology, myth and ethics. For this reason 'winning the hearts and minds' of a people is a complex business. In a sense it cannot be done, for predispositions must already be there. But a doctrine, such as that of social democracy, can have a very powerful appeal in some circumstances to those who have not yet experienced it. We see how Spain and Portugal, who never had experienced it, are now trying it out, and seem for the time being to have rejected harsher doctrines of both right and left.

But the main burden of what I want to say is that any universal doctrine is likely to be in conflict with the nationalism it under-pins. But it is easy to be blind to this, and national religious or ideological worldviews are dangerous to morality, for they give moral reasons for doing the most atrocious things. Here I am already making the transition to value-judgments, so let me now add some observations about a possible Christian evaluation of nationalism.

II

First, I think it is important to stress a characteristic of Christianity which in a sense goes beyond its universalism, namely the way in which it incorporates and points to the Transcendent. But it is of course the testimony of much of modernity that the belief in transcendence is only a *possibility*. The old proofs have long since softened and some have melted away. The old authority of rev-elation has fragmented in a hermeneutical and institutional kal-eidoscope. A new epistomology looks towards criticism and the uses of imagination, of the fragility indeed even of the received edifices of science. The history of religions has opened up a plethora of alternatives. The open society is one where people are free to change worldviews. It is no wonder that philosophers of religion have favoured often doctrines which see religious belief as grounded in alternative vision or insulated faith.

Inevitably, all this means that belief in the Transcendent cannot be affirmed dogmatically. But if we are Christians then neither should it be sacrificed. It was unfortunate that some exponents of the secular theology of the 1960s were unclear on this: taking non-religious values seriously does not entail giving up Transcendence. For one thing, of course, belief in the Transcendent in taking us beyond the world leaves the world where it is: it is its own cure for supersitition.

But where does this leave the Christian? And what is the application to the question of nationalism? I say this: belief in the Transcendent takes us to a point from which we can, so to speak beyond the world, criticize the world. It represents the place from which the world can be seen, and how it is seen is due to the colouration of the Transcendent given by the teachings, myth and practice of Christian faith. So now Chistian doctrines become, not a set of dogmas, but a framework for critiquing our world, including within it nationalism.

As science too is a matter of criticism, theorizing, imagination – so too a critical component is a necessary feature of Christian living. This is how our epistemology can be both soft and vigorous.

Such Neotranscendentalism as I like to call it is so far, however, merely a formal position. What materially has to be the content of criticism and evaluation of nationalism and the nation-State?

In moving to a second step, I should like to say how it is that even from the formal position one can infer some material consequences. If the soft character of religious and more generally worldview epistemology is established, and every position is essentially open to debate, then it seems unreasonable to impose any point of view. Good education would be peppered with maybes. Worldview education should in principle be plural. So a values pluralism would itself be a value: a surer value than the others. So soft epistemology is a reason for pluralistic toleration, and so the impartial State.

But the Christian has a calling too: she has a vision of the world and of what lies Beyond that inspires her to enthusiasm with openness. Softness is not the same as relativism, and non-relativistic positions may be occupied with passion.

The position of official impartiality, and the fact of soft non-relativism, together seem to point to a conclusion that every grouping will become in principle a voluntary one. It is true that it is impossible to escape the milieu of early education, the way we are brought up: this imprints Chineseness or Scottishness or whatever into our wiring. But we can free ourselves gradually of these imprintings, and that is partly what we mean by the possibility of conversion. Because I am Scottish I do not need to label myself as such.

It thus seems to be that in varying degree our collectivities become voluntary ones – or at least the collectivities which express and mould worldviews. This does not mean that national identities are unimportant, because they are important to people, and within limits what is important or dear to others should secondarily be important or dear to me, just because other people are important or dear to me. Love thy neighbour, then secondarily respect his cat.

As a secondary good the nation-State can be a blessing up to a point. It conduces somewhat to cultural variation, it is an agent of various forms of welfare, and so on. The deprivation of national autonomy can be sociopsychologically embittering, and so liberation movements in general have a secondary validity. But the liberation of a collectivity is compatible, as we know, with the deprivation of individual freedoms. There is, however, an argument that we should support national independence or autonomy wherever feasible, not as an end in itself, but as one step towards human dignity. For obvious reasons, the individualism of world citizenship is not appealing to national liberators.

Nothing, however, that I have so far affirmed, it will be said, is Christian as such. It could as easily be affirmed by a humanist. But I take it as obvious that human dignity and freedom are also Christian values, and that if there is any collectivity to which the Christian has ultimate loyalty it is not the nation, but either the Church or humanity as a whole. It seems indeed plausible to hold that the Christian's ultimate group is humanity, seen of course as possessing the imprint of the divine image. The Church, which I take to be constituted by some large segment of world Christianity, is a source of power for the Christian, and could thus be described as a divine transnational corporation in the service (of Christ of course and) humanity.

From this perspective, what role is left for nationalism? In one form it seems that it can be recognized as having conventional or provisional validity. The form is defensive or federal nationalism. There is no case for aggrandizing nationalism – the nationalism of empires; and internal minorities thus have to be treated with special tenderness, or a nation-State may be committing internal aggression. There are many examples of this. I think the lesson is the extension of the federal or cantonal principle. There are also so many cases where national self-determination is denied because a people straddles frontiers, such as the Kurdish question. It seems to me moreover that there remains a severe problem about how we deal with mingled populations, such as Indians and Fijians in Fiji, Sinhala and Tamils in Sri Lanka, Protestants and Catholics in Ireland and so on. Such populations are growing, and the nationalism of the dominant group often helps to aggravate ethnic relations. Such ethnic mixes often are where one main element is a diaspora: and we need more consideration of the role and nature of diasporas in the world. On balance, modern times have shown that ethnic groups have great difficulty living reasonably and peacefully together. Racism, ethnicism and various forms of groupism are endemic to the human condition. Sometimes Americans do not see this as clearly because America has its own solution: baptizing everyone into a new community so to speak, in which there is a myth which can give meaning to minorities. But most nations are not blessed with the myths or even the vocabulary for the melting pot.

Religions as transnational groups, and Christianity in particular with its myth of neither-Jew-nor-Greek, etc., can thus help to spread a kind of provisional federalism about groups, and above all national and ethnic groups.

In certain respects, the importance of the national group is diminishing. The economics of the world has in the last two decades made immense strides towards being genuinely global. This is not to everyone's satisfaction, because exploitation and poverty are not thereby diminished. But it means that if there is a sort of economic imperialism it is not at all like those of the past: for the transnational corporations are themselves in process of becoming non-national. It is so to say an imperialism without a country. It is neocapitalism as a global system. Khieu Sampan was correct in thinking that to contract out you have to become rural and autarkic, and the consequences of that experiment were terrifying. So it is virtually impossible to avoid the new global system. Socialist countries are part of it too: sometimes using their internal repressive power to keep wages down so that transnationals could profit thereby. ˇ

The new, however, is not all bad, for transnationals are immensely productive, do not possess except by proxy the instruments of war and internal terror, and prefer an internationalist ideology to justify their operations. But neocapitalism, though it profits by State socialism sometimes, cannot really approve it: it is not interested in barriers, and Communist states erect the highest barriers. The danger is that transnational neocapitalism can combine with a kind of chauvinistic nationalism to produce a Zoroastrian theology of present world history.

The transnationals seem to me then to create a new role for the nation-State. That is as a kind of union, to moderate the impact of transnational and global capitalism. If the employer is transnational, the union has to be so – and the only effective unit is States in combination.

Now Christianity, self-evidently, is, like other faiths, concerned with compassion: and perhaps more intensely in the modern period feels the call of social concerns. The problems of modern poverty exist above all in a global context: to a great extent, but not completely, the so-called developed countries have eliminated the worst poverty, especially in social democracies like Sweden and New Zealand. Northern poverty is there and is a misery, but it is nothing compared with the poverty of much of the South. Generally speaking the most potent way of combining individual freedom and social compassion has been through social democracy. Indeed it seems to me hard to avoid thinking of it as the most compatible political ideology for the Christian. Caught in the trap of some particular country where its realization is remote the Christian might support other causes, but ultimately the ideal of the caring community seems best expressed where freedom and compassion combine. Consequently, by a transposition to the global level it seems to me evident that here too the policy should be a kind of global social democracy – in line somewhat with the thinking of the Brandt Commission.

But life will not improve ultimately for our fellow humans if the only transnationals are corporations and economic communities. Where is the soul of the world? The religions too are transnationals. As I have argued, the Christian faith now stands as critic of the world – critic of the smugness of the affluent, the cruelty of dictators, the divisiveness of ethnicity. In regard to the latter my main thesis has been that the nation is at best a secondary haven. The nation should not be allowed to be the group of ultimate concern. Combining religion and State, or ideology and State, is a way of doing just that: giving ultimacy to the State. The only civil religion worth having is kenotic.

The tests of global policy are clear enough it seems: Does it reduce violence, does it increase affluence and distribute fairly, does it increase individual dignity, does it have humanity as its group of ultimate concern? The nation-State is a convenience for helping in these goals, but only at the price of admitting a kind of global federalism. Most of our institutions are ill-adapted to this: so the Christian as a transnational citizen of heaven must be a severe and relentless critic of the nationalist religion when it becomes absolute.

5

Resurgence and Identity in Three Faiths

The resurgences growing today in some areas of the three faiths Judaism, Christianity and Islam are responses to forces, both soft and harsh, which, in threatening and changing life as earlier conceived, seem to make it imperative to assert new forms of religious and ideological identity. I think it is important, if we are to reflect about such phenomena as the Gush Emunim, the Moral Majority and the Muslim Brotherhood, not to be trapped by preconceived Western categories. In particular, we ought to be clear about how we are to think about religion itself. I wish therefore to begin by some reflections about the categories we bring to bear on our theme. Then secondly I shall try to sketch in broad lines the living context in which the three traditions find themselves in the modern world. And then I hope to analyse some of the human facts of the resurgences, and think a bit about what the future holds in store.

Although we are used in the West to a strong line drawn between religion and politics, this line (whatever we think of it – whether we be vigorous defenders of such separation or not) is itself a value-position. It involves a certain ideological stance. It seems to me more realistic to recognize that religious and political worldviews belong on the same spectrum, and that in studying religion as a separate entity we are unnecessarily confining the scope of our understanding. What is clearer is that human beings have certain beliefs, modes of acting, institutions and so on which are sometimes traditionally religious (and thus incorporate ritual activity and a belief in the transcendent) and sometimes are expressed in a more secular mode. I therefore conceive our task in the study of religion to be something which ought to be described more broadly. The task of describing and trying to understand belief-systems and practical orientations to life I would like to call *worldview analysis*.[1] One advantage of this is that we may come to see some of the styles of resurgence that we are considering in a new light, namely as blends of worldview – for instance blending motifs drawn from traditional religion with part of the modern ideology of nationalism, and so on. This is important, incidentally for the conversation of the disciplines. The historian of religions, the anthropologist, the sociologist, the political scientist, the economist, the area specialist – they are all dealing with the same complex whole in analysing the forces of modern Egypt or today's Sri Lanka. In particular, it strikes me that worldview analysis is a viable and important area of the curriculum and of research which is rather unnaturally carved up between religious studies, political science, philosophy, anthropology and so on. If the systematic study of economic behaviour is important, then so is the systematic study of beliefs and values across the board.

The upshot, though, of my primary thought in regard to religions and worldviews is that typically each religious or other worldview is a kind of syncretism, or at least a blend of motifs. And this may help us to reflect more clearly about the kinds of religious resurgence with which we are mainly concerned.

Let us now stand back a little to look to the broader milieu of the three faiths in the modern world. Of course in speaking of three faiths I really mean many more, for each faith comes in so many varieties: we are wise to think not of Judaism, Christianity and Islam but of Judaisms, Christianities, Islams. Descriptively they are many however much they may (and they do not always) look to some kind of normative unity. It is best to begin with the context of Christianity, because it is the most important religion of the Western world, and it is the West which has been the main setter of the agenda for the rest of the world in the last three hundred years or more.

Perhaps the single most important force in modern Western development in the last two hundred years has been nationalism. It created its own powerful loyalties, and produced units of population large enough for the processes of modernization and industrialization to occur. Intermediate units tended to be erased, while the demands of national unity made for novel forms of myth (i.e. the nation's history), ritual (anthems, military displays), ethics (those of loyal and useful citizenship) and institutional transmission (such as the educational systems brought into being in the latter half of the 19th century). National music, poets, thinkers and painters helped to express national spirit.[2] Given appetites stimulated by economic growth, the nationalisms of Europe often turned into imperialisms, and thereby transmitted by counter-suggestibility bred of psychic and real wounds nationalism in other areas of the world. To some extent Christianity functioned as part of the ideology of Western imperialisms, although nationalism itself tended to erode or even to struggle consciously against old Church-State solidarity.

Nationalism will engage our attention later: for patriotism is an ingredient in the thinking of the Moral Majority, the whole question of Israel's nature and role arises out of the nationalist milieu, and resurgent Islam, while not precisely displaying nationalist elements in the more typical Western sense, is in part a nationalist-type response to the Western incursion into the fabric of Islam.

The West was also the bosom for the arising of modern critical and scientific ways of understanding the world. Of course, the critical scientific method is no more in essence Western than is cheese, but it happens to be a product of the West, now become more universal. This provided a new worldview, both because the content of science changed our cosmology, but also because the critical and experimental method implicitly called in question older authorities. This bred the agnostic attitude to religious truth which came to be so powerful an ingredient in modern humanism.

The technological fruits of critical scientism and modern industrial society raised the question in the minds of a number of cultures as to whether one could have the technology grafted onto the tradition without buying into the critical scientism and humanist values exhibited by elite Western culture. This was rendered the more acture because in practice critical scientism was wedded to liberal individualism.

This major ingredient in Western culture was of Christian parentage in part – fruit of the radical Reformation; but it was also a product of the Enlightenment and of utilitarian economics. The freedom of each person was blended with the paradoxical notion that each person can be seen as a unit, for purposes of production and consumption. Paradoxical, because individualism simultaneously stresses the uniqueness and interchangeability of each individual.

With liberal individualism came increased emphasis on choice, and so a relatively permissive ethos. Intellectually it could combine with critical scientism in challenging much of the traditional worldview of Christianity, though it could also combine with Christian values, as liberal Protestantism, and with Jewish values as Reform Judaism.

One other motif of modern worldviews must be mentioned – the socialist tradition, itself bifurcating into two streams – one blending with liberal values and becoming social democracy, the other the Marxist, more holistic and authoritarian strand. Both could blend easily with nationalism, and even with in effect an imperial stance – in the Soviet Union – to become the national Marxisms of today.

These in brief are the varied soft and harsh forces which relate to questions of identity that help to explain some of the conservative resurgences of the contemporary world.

For the West, by spreading its power during the colonial phase into the Islamic world, and by continuing later through the capitalist system and through political means since World War II and the end of the colonial era, has brought these forces into every Islamic country. And the West too, by releasing from within itself the secluded forces of an older Judaism, and then by both negatively, through the Holocaust, and positively through a certain degree of political support, creating and sustaining the State of Israel, has forced upon Judaism choices relating to these modern worldview motifs.

The three religions have however a very different placement. The West consists in a loose coalition of largely social democratic and liberal nations; but they are bound together not primarily by conscious adherence to Christian values, though they are an important ingredient in the pluralistic mix. Since much of the success of the West is seen in terms of scientific and technological power, and its preferred ideological value is individualism, there is some tension between its democratic values and those of the Christian traditions. It is true that liberal Protestants and increasingly Catholics of the Aggiornamento have woven a tapestry of Christian personalism and social concern which can blend Western and traditional worldviews. But there are tensions. Moreover there are non-Christian religious motifs in the plural West which increasingly make themselves felt: not just Judaism, but also Eastern religions, reinforced by the fact that Japan and other honorary Western nations of Asia manage to blend Zen or Confucius with business economics.

By contrast, the unity of the Islamic countries – such as it is – owes itself to a consciousness of traditional Islam. And in the Arab countries the sense of separate nationalism is less important than in comparable countries of the West. Throughout the Islamic world the major national struggle has been against the West (with such exceptions as the Iraq–Iran war), and Islamic values thus become central to national consciousness. So there is a degree to which the Islamic countries identify themselves in terms of an underlying Islamic civilization: and this contrasts with the West where the consciousness is more of modernity and freedom than of an underlying Christian civilization. It is true that Christianity functioned as part of the ideology of conquest during the imperial phase; but this notion of a 'Christian civilization' is much more muted today. It is a nostalgia among some Christians, however, and this is relevant to our theme.

Judaism is in a third category. It is of course both a diaspora and a nation: or rather the religious and secular values of the tradition and its modern products are incarnated as diaspora and nation-State. Since the diaspora is most importantly found in the social democratic and liberal West, Judaism follows some Christian options in the range from liberal interpretation through to self-conscious traditionalism. But in Israel it has to face nationalism in a very special form. Its options are difficult. On the one hand there is the social-democratic, critical-scientific modernizing nationalism of the Herzl mode and Zionist movement; on the other hand, there are traditionalist options which are in tension with such a 'modern' Israel. Part of the function of right wing religious movements is to effect a synthesis between nationalism and traditionalism.

Since the placement of the three religious traditions is so different, the neotraditionalism in each case has to solve rather different problems. The Western fundamenalist Christian solves mainly the problem of individual identity within an atomistic individualist environment. He presents a message relevant to the welfare of individuals struggling within a wider society which, in at least appealing to freedom of choice, had eroded authority. The Biblical preacher is able to stir a sense of Biblical inerrancy which guarantees the validity of values others had put into jeopardy. Moreover, in emphasizing the family and the nation it offered assurance of at least some stability and power within these most basic communities. Because it is a creed preached in an individualistic society the engines of solidarity themselves turn out to be individual – the response of the 'born again' person, who feels the truth within her or his own immediate experience. Thus though the new fundamentalism does prescribe a moral code, it is essentially concerned with inner commitment.

The 'fundamentalist' aspect of the teaching is significant because it by rejecting liberalism and thus the critical–scientific attitude in relation to the Bible itself resolves doubt. Critical–scientific attitudes are dangerous as individualism also in creating so much room for choice that confusion and meaninglessness set in. At the same time the general tendency towards patriotism in the Moral Majority helps to reinforce meaning from another direction: by participating in a great nation each individual shares greatness.[3] However, the extra meaning is bought at a certain expense: Biblical literalism implies epistemological remoteness from much of the more educated population, and creates an uncomfortable rift between science and religion. Yet this is not immediately apparent to the faithful, because undoubtedly neo-fundamentalism is modernistic in its use of technology, and for those who think that science is technology (and not critical and imaginative experimental and theoretical procedures) there can be a blend of pre-scientific and scientific (i.e. technological) attitudes.

In this fundamentalists can be compared to their counterparts in Islam. It is a theme of many writers including the Ayatollah Khomeini that it is possible to blend Islam and science (conceived essentially as technology) without introducing perverted liberal ideas from the West.[4] A lot depends, in estimating the long-term prospects of this position, on whether critical methodology can be isolated strictly within the bounds of purely scientific specu-lation: or whether alternatively science needs for its success a generally open society.

This is no theoretical question, for it is strongly relevant to the chief question animating so many modern Muslims: how is it that the true faith and its civilization are still in such an unflourishing condition? How is it that Islam is still less successful in worldly terms than is the decadent West? What can be done to revive Islamic culture?[5].

One answer of course has been to change the question – and think instead about Turkish or Arab culture. Then it becomes possible to think that we can get rid of Islam itself, or at least we can tame it, and by Westernizing achieve the same riches and power as the West has. Such a radically secularizing policy was of course tried in Turkey. Somewhat similar ideas have been tried out through varieties of Arab socialism. But over the last fifty years the importation of Western modernizations, such as political and legal institutions, has not marked great success. From this perspective, there can be disillusionment with either substitutions of Islam or Westernizing modernizations of Islam. Hence the attractions of traditionalism.

This states: our troubles stem from the fact that we have not been Muslim enough: we have not followed God's law or been loyal enough to the tradition. Thus Islam's apparent lack of success relatively to the West is a sign of divine judgment upon the not-so-faithful. But can the answer then be just going back to traditional Islam as though nothing had happened? Far from it. The more powerful movements in Islam today are one way or another not just traditionalist: they are self-consciously traditional but in a new key. In a word, they are neotraditionalist, just as the Christian fundamentalist is. And what does the 'neo' consist of?

It consists in taking important elements from the invading cultural forces and adapting them to Islamic ideals. Thus modern banking, technology and business methods are taken over in a manner made to conform with Islamic law in Khomeini's Iran. Moreover, the idea of an Islamic Republic is itself a blend of older Islamic ideas of Islamic political community and the style of the modern nation-State. Similarly the vision of the future conveyed in the writings of Hasan Al-Bannā was one of a reconstituted Islamic community flourishing through a strict moral code and the use of modern technology of all kinds.

It is worth remarking here that it is above all in colleges and universities, even outside Islamic culture, that the ideals of Islamic brotherhood and revival of this neotraditionalist mode are most in evidence.[6] The appeal of fundamentalism is here to the relatively well educated: the converse is true of Christian fundamentalism, on the whole.

Often such neotraditionalism is as strongly critical of traditionalists as it is of foreign influence. This is evident too in literature of the Ikhwan (the Muslim Brotherhood). Thus Saudi Arabia often comes in for criticism, despite its apparently traditionalist Wahhabi regime, in that it has failed to integrate Islam and the practice of the State: the Western elements in the State thus become grounds of corruption.

While within the American context it is possible for the Moral Majority to be nationalist in a fairly straightforward way,[7] Islam is essentially transnational. Thus there were seeds of conflict between the Brotherhood and Nasser and Sadat, because these had come to practice Egyptian as well as more broadly Arab nationalism, and so were turning Egypt into a 'modern' State. In principle also therefore Khomeini's revolution is for export throughout the world of Islam (and he is of course a popular rallying point of anti-Western Islamic revivalism).

The difference between Christian revivalism and Islamic lies thus in part in the very different placements. However much the member of the evangelical wing of Christianity may come to distrust liberalism and its fruits, he or she very squarely rests upon values taken to be essential to the home tradition. Some of these values, even the conservative ones, are alien to the Muslim. The struggle between tradition and liberalism, etc. is in an Islamic context in part the struggle between what is home grown and what is foreign. Thus xenophobia has its place in Islamic revivalism.

Part of this xenophobia relates, of course, to Israel perceived as a Zionist entity intruding wrongly into the territory of Islam.[8] Zion has of course a very different role to play in much Christian fundamentalism.

As I have indicated more than once, there is a stronger sense of Islamic civilization, over against both Marxism and the West, than there is of a Christian civilization. It is implicit in Islamic revival that Islam transcends nations, which are just the tribes of old writ large. Thus potentially such revival is dangerous to states that have established a strong ideology of the nation, such as socialist Algeria, even Ghaddafi's Libya and secularist Syria and Iraq. Modern conditions favour this Panislamic revivalism. It is easier to go on Hajj. Publications can circulate easily in the Muslim world, and the very power of Western ideas and institutions can create by contrast a sense of Islamic unity. There is nothing comparable in the Christian case. If anything Christianity has tended to become rather many-nationed, so that Christianity goes with patriotism, and there are many patriotisms. If anything it is liberal Christianity rather than conservative forms which is –

through for example the ecumenical movement – more trans-national in orientation.

One other comment by way of comparison and contrast between Christian and Islamic fundamentalism – before I turn to the case of Judaism. Though the word 'fundamentalism' is rather loosely used of Islamic neotraditionalism, it conceals an important difference of attitude. For the Christian the Book may be inerrant, but behind it lies Jesus: that is where the ultimate locus of faith and authority lies. But in Islam the Qur'an is more like an incarnation. Its eternal status gives it a much more immovable character and divinely magical quality than even the fun-damentalist's Bible can have. This bears on the unwillingness to even think about critical questions and gives Islamic neo-traditionalism a great power and definition.

If conservative Christianity in the West adapts naturally to various patriotisms; and if neotraditional Islam is in principle transnational; Judaism has a special tie to one particular nation. If Christian revival tends to recreate the individual and a sense of belonging, and Islamic revival seeks to recreate a divine civi-lization, religious Zionism seeks to recreate a holy nation. Thus the Gush Emunim represent one natural option of belief given the foundation of the State of Israel.

If we cast our thoughts back to the forces which I sketched near the beginning – including nationalism, socialism and liberal individualism, plus science and technology – these obviously had their effects on Judaism as on other forms of religion. It happens that a version of the mixture between individualism, critical sci-entism, socialism and nationalism was in the heritage of the Zionist movement. But the nationalist ingredient could operate in the opposite direction, not impelling the Jew towards his own nationalism, but assimilating him in the patriotisms of Germany, or France, or the United States. Actually, there can be an inter-esting relationship between secular Israel nationalism and liberal or secular assimilation to other nationalisms: Israel becomes as it were a secular anchor for a secularized diaspora. But becoming a religious anchor for the religious diaspora proves a bit more complicated, in so far as the foundation of the State did not fit with the eschatological expectations regarding the Messiah. This is where a neotraditional rather aggressive religious nationalism for Israel, as expressed by Gush Emunim among others, helps to synthesize the religious and secular aspirations of the State.[9]

In the above analyses of the differing situations of the religions I have of course been highly selective. I have said nothing about ecumenical revival in Christianity or the multitudinous new Christian movements in Africa and elsewhere. I have looked to the Ikhwan, but have said nothing about revived Islamic forces in Malaysia,[10] Pakistan[11] or elsewhere, nor about Mahdist and other extreme movements in Northern Nigeria or among those who took over the great Mosque at Mecca.[12] And I have said nothing about the varied vitality of mainstream Jewish movements. And here it is also useful to add something on the religious and spiritual meaning of some of these new searches for identity.

The sentiments, of course, which enter into such searches are a blend, but they include the sense of relationship to God, nurtured in differing ways – by the intensity of Islamic prayer, the Torah as constant reminder and means of expressing loyalty, and prayer with Jesus. Because of these emotional and ritual aspects of traditional religion, the latter has a great power to mobilize individual loyalty and meaning. Whatever we might think ultimately about the neotraditional resurgence, its capacity to channel such sentiments and to use them is an indication of the continuing vitality of religious experience.

Frankly, I think all the resurgences contain unresolved contradictions. For neotraditional Islam the roots of scientific and other creativity have not been I think properly perceived – they are found in a degree of liberty and non-conformism, as well as international cooperation, hard to conceive in revived traditional Islam. For the Moral Majority, there is the tension between this quest for meaning and the pluralism which allows others their quest for meaning; and the tension between Christian universal feeling and the reliance on the patriotic community. For religious Judaism in Israel there remains ultimately, as for all Israelis, the contradiction between the ideals of the new State and the actual condition of non-Jewish citizens.

But all the cases we have looked at reflect elements in the doctrines of the three religions. These monotheists have such different Gods. The revival movements maintain each its hard epistemology, as though it is known which of these Gods is the true one. This is the intellectual reflection of a strong desire for defined community. One of the major issues of our world of course is to do with the rules, epistemological and otherwise, which allow such communities to live together.

It is hazardous to predict how the future will develop. I am inclined to think that Christian fundamentalism, however important in the United States, remains somewhat marginal in the world as a whole, not only because transnational Christianity is represented in its mainstream by the ecumenical movement, including post-Vatican II Catholicism, but also because right wing politics are not attractive (in their White form) to Third World Christians. But by contrast, Islamic fundamentalism is of the main stream. The processes of interaction across the Muslim world and of the growth of Panislamic consciousness are by no means waning. On the contrary, the multiplication of Western influence through global economics and the media are likely to stimulate it further. Xenophobia is created most by the presence, not the absence, of the *xenon*. All this may point to continued revivalism, the instability of acculturating regimes, and a bitterer conflict ultimately, despite the present signs, over Palestine.

6

The Dynamics of Religious and Political Change: Illustrations from South Asia

The aim of this paper is to sketch a programme, and to delineate the bones of a theory, and to hint at the flesh thereof by examples drawn from South Asia. The programme is to develop a dynamic phenomenology. That is, it is to find ways of adding to the static typology of classical history of religions, approaches a *typology of changes*: to see rituals and doctrines and myths and institutions in motion. It thus has analogies to work in the sociology of knowledge, and owes much to the example of Weber. But my interest is not merely social, though it is partly that. It is a concern with the six or seven dimensions of religion, with doctrine, myth, ethics, experience, ritual and aesthetic objects as well as the social aspect and milieu of religion. So it is intentionally a *dynamic typology* from the direction of the history of religions.

It is also, though not only, concerned with religions as traditionally understood. It is simply not realistic for us to draw a sharp line between religion and non-religion, between religions and ideologies, between religions and quasi-religions. This is so for three reasons. First, and least importantly, the very definition of religion is controversial and scarcely clear. Second, even if we draw a line (for instance in terms of the notion of transcendence or through the identification of 'typical' types of religious experience) there are plenty of resemblances in the other dimensions between religions and ideologies. Third, most importantly of all, and I hope to illustrate this in this paper, in fact many modern movements are blends or syncretisms of religious and ideological themes: thus Lech Walesa's worldview blends Catholicism and

Polish nationalism; Christian liberation theology blends Christian and Marxist themes, and so on. For a proper analysis of world-views we need realistically to stretch our dimensions well beyond what is by a strict definition 'religious'.

So my project differs from some previous ways of doing phenomenology in being *dynamic* and *transreligious*: going beyond religion as such. That is why I sometimes like to refer to the descriptive side of our field as *worldview* analysis: here then I offer some reflections on dynamic worldview analysis.

And what is the point of doing it? Better to understand the ways our world works: that is the primary concern. Underlying it is a thought which I can express as follows: that ideas, feelings, performances, experiences have powerful effects in the human world, and so the history of consciousness is vital for the under-standing of changes in the world. Too often modern thinking has gone the other way, as though religions and ideologies are merely epiphenomenal, and as though the 'real' changes have economic and technological motors. Well of course they do, but they have mental motors too. Behind each technology there are minds. Was not the moon landing an ideological as well as a scientific fact?

For these and other reasons our field, especially if stretched into sisterly fields as worldview analysis, is a core activity in understanding the human condition. Of course we may often be more concerned with the individual quest for faith and enlight-enment within the deerpark of the religions and ideologies, rather than the more macroscopic changes with which I am here concerned. But even individual questing takes place in a wider political and spiritual world which we as individual seekers need to take cognizance of. So much for an *apologia pro phenomenologia mea*.

I wish in this chapter to use, as I have said, examples from South Asia, primarily from India and Sri Lanka. Like other regions of the world it has had to pass through the traumatic period of Western expansion and conquest. This can roughly be divided into the colonial and postcolonial phases, the latter characterized by the emergence of a transnational but still rather Western-dominated global economic system, within which Marxist coun-tries operate as partly antagonistic elements. But at any rate South Asian cultures have been faced by the complexities of Western ideas and influences. As elsewhere the most vital transactions of the mind and heart have been across this cultural interface, an interface I like to call the White Frontier. In the modern period therefore many of the changing factors have been related to the West, and what best psychic and political deals can be made with the great intruders: colonialism, nationalism, scientism, modern Christian missions, utilitarianism, democracy, socialism, industrialism.

It may be noted that a significant new branch in the history of religions is the study of new religious movements in primal or small-scale societies, a field pioneered by Harold Turner. At the same time there is much interest in new religious movements in the West. There is perhaps a growing realization that we need a global approach to varieties of new religions and ideologies, many of which arise from cultural interaction and above *all* from the need to adjust to the vast new secular forces both outside and inside the West of modern science, industry, capitalism and so on. (One may note that there is also a White Frontier within the white countries: the frontier between the new global forces and religious tradition, so from this point of view new Western religious movements and forms of revivalism are analogous to those changes set off beyond the White Frontier by the impact of modernity on on-Western societies).

I also need by way of a preliminary to introduce into my treatment the notions of particularity, types of themes, and the idea of more or less organic collage. Let me illustrate from Theravada Buddhism in Sri Lanka. First, a religion such as this has much that is very particular: location in a particular geography, that of Sri Lanka, the appeal to a particular historical figure, Gotama, the particular character of Pali and Sinhala as languages, and so on. But there are types too of a more general thematic significance. The Sangha represents a form of monastic organization, the saffron robe is a kind of sacred dress, the fasting after noon is a kind of moderate austerity, the offering of flowers to Buddha statutes is a kind of *puja*, the practice of meditation is a type of yoga, the cult of Kataragama involves a variety of pilgrimage, the concept of nibbana is a notion of transcendence, the story of the Buddha is a version of the story of the spiritual hero . . . and so on. Thus in the Theravada various particularities and themes are brought together in a more or less *organic collage*. Every religious system can be seen like this, as a collage and as organic in the sense that the meaning of each element is partly affected by the rest of the system, just as the function and nature of a horse's hind leg is affected by the disposition and functioning of the rest of the animal. So the meaning of monasticism is related to the Buddha's foundational intentions, which is affected by the doctrine of rebirth, and so on.

Clearly, the impact of intruding cultural elements can have the effect of adding themes to the total cultural environment, and the result is that the tradition may try to work some of them into its collage: by the principle of *organic contextuality* that itself is going to affect to a greater or lesser degree the meaning of the traditional elements in the collage. This observation will prove important when we come to look more deeply into the dynamic phenomenology of India.

Another general observation of importance for my theme is that part of the modern condition, though not exclusive to it, is a sense of the *historical past*. History as we tell it often indeed functions as *myth*, giving us a sense of where our values came from, celebrating ancestors and so forth. Now by using modern categories about the past we are already subtly or not so subtly changing it. Consider talk of 'India', for instance. We have a notion of the India of the Raj as a geographic unit and project that back into the past, and so come to speak of Indian history. Maybe in some ways it is not too misleading, but it paves the path to various modes of rearranging the past. As I like to say: for a new religion Hinduism has remarkably ancient roots. This points to ways in which Hindus and non-Hindus alike may reshape the story of the sub-continent's spirituality.

And to complicate life further we ourselves (whoever we are, but I am now identifying ourselves as those involved in the exploration of the human religious–ideological past) make contributions which themselves have an effect on worldview self-consciousness. This is how the study of any X can have, if X be human, a reflexive effect upon X itself. It is the quantum physics of the cultural milieu.

I have delineated a religious tradition or subtradition as a kind of collage in which various particularities and thematic elements are held together and, so to speak, interwoven contextually. In the case of the deep Indian tradition there is a whole mass of themes which have been interwoven in any number of contextual collages. Of these classical Hinduism is a subset. Buddhism, Jainism and so on represent other subsets. And not only with the coming of the White Frontier (and before that the Islamic Frontier) various of the traditions, already in motion together, have been stimulated to new changes. Moreoever, we can even see in the new situation the way *thematic elements themselves* can under go phenomenological changes. There is for instance the history of the guru-across-the-White-Frontier, of bhakti and yoga as export items, so to say, of technological changes to pilgrimage, etc. Themes can be detached from their traditional collage and embedded in other ones. Before I can sketch some of the ways the traditions have responded to modernity, let me list some of what I consider to be the major themes or typical elements of the Indian tradition (and here I mean primarily the Hindu traditions, Indian Buddhist ones, Jainism, etc.: I leave on one side Inidan Islam, Zoroastrianism, etc.). So then some themes, not in order of importance:

a *bhakti* mode;
a yoga mode;
rebirth doctrine;
a theory of merit;
the recognition of holy men, recluses, ascetics, etc.; a widespread sacred priestly class;
monasticism;
the pursuit of liberation;
ideas of dharma;
a mass of mythic material;
images, ikons, temples;
holy places;
ancient scriptural traditions;
secondary scriptural traditions;
traditional systems of learning and philosophy;
the figure of the teacher or guru;
the concept of ethical conduct built into the fabric of the cosmos;
the picture of a pulsating cosmos;
sacramental rituals;
tantric motifs and rites;
household rituals;
notions of purity and impurity;
the veneration of the cow;
astrology as a mode of determining auspicious times etc.
a hierarchical mosaic of social groups;
austerities;

pilgrimage;
a pluralism of gods;
a sense of divine unity;
a theological tradition or set of traditions, Vedānta;
regional theological variations, e.g. S'aiva Siddhānta;
new movements reinterpreting tradition in modern times.

Clearly some of these themes are more important in some sub-traditions and traditions than others: e.g. the theologies are not important in Theravada Buddhism. Sometimes the themes have a subordinate place, e.g. the gods in Buddhism. Again *bhakti* is important for Ramanuja, but not particularly for Patanjali.

Indianness, as expressed through a loose federation of practices and institutions exhibiting various blends of the above themes, was faced under the Raj with a number of external motifs, which can be listed as follows, each representing a distinctive challenge to what had gone before:

a more or less unitary foreign rule;
Western Orientalism;
industrial capitalism;
utilitarianism and ideas of liberal democracy;
Western science;
evangelicalism and other forms of Christianity;
the concept of nationalism;
British-style education, especially universities.

The first major revolt against some of these themes was largely blind and inarticulate: the events of 1857. But soon something much better worked out came to dominate the scene in India itself. This was what can be called the modern Hindu ideology, which was a synthesis lending itself to responses to some of the more important challenges listed above. In Sri Lanka things were rather different and for the moment I shall concentrate on the Indian scene.

One of the most important tasks for those who wished to deal with the intruders was to interpret history. Generally we can see a history of a religion as divided into four main phases: the primordial, the post-primordial, the classical phase and a modern phase. If you are a Muslim, then the period of the Qur'an and the prophet is primordial; the first four Khalifs or so represent

the post-primordial phase; the golden age of empires and synthesis the classical; and the period from Napoleon onwards the
modern period. For the Hindu the Vedas can be seen as primordial; the Hinduism of castes, temples, bhakti, images, and the
whole federated congeries of thematic elements listed above can
be seen as classical; and the time from Akbar until now as the
modern period. The weakening of a tradition in the encounter
with the White Frontier may be ascribed to a corrupt past, and
so one option in reforming the tradition in the face of the challenge may be to reject the classical and modern phases, in favour
of a return either to the primordial or to the post-primordial at
least. We can see these moves at work in some of the new
movements of 19th century Hinduism (but note some Muslim
cases; both the Wahhabi and Gaddafi are 'primordialists', the
Ayatollah a version of post-primordialist, and in all these cases
external themes are absorbed into the fabric of a 'fundamentalist'
worldview). Thus: Raja Ram Mohan Roy's Brahmo Samaj can be
seen as incorporating early motifs but rejecting classical Hinduism
for the most part. On the other hand, the Arya Samaj is pri-
mordialist, and effectively rejects the Hinduism of the Gita
onwards, save for those Brahmanical motifs which fit a slimmed,
reform Hinduism. Both movements were aniconic and mono-
theistic, but within a Hindu framework. They thus effected one
particular synthesis or blend between the old and the intruding
faith. But it was the *modern Hindu ideology* of Vivekananda and
others that proved most effective as a blend, because it incor-
porated most of the elements of both the old and the incoming
tradition. Let me look at it from the point of view of how this
neo-Vedanta could deal with the Western themes I have listed.
(a) It could cope with Western Orientalism by seeing the Hindu
tradition as both classical and as having ancient roots. The scriptures could be seen as testifying to an unfolding evolution of
religious consciousness, and particularly the Neo-Advaitin concept of levels of truth could cope with the Orientalist erosion of
a monolithic view of *śruti*. In fact the Advaitin view was not
altogether different in principle from Barth's distinction between
the levels of the self-revelatory Gospel on the one hand and of
the human religious response on the other. (b) Similarly the
Vendantin doctrine of *śabda* or testimony could in effect define
the difference between the realm of the Transcendent and the
cosmic realm to which the sciences apply. So there need be no

clash between Western science and traditional religious experience. Incidentally, the very different Indian feel about animals largely accounts for the lack of hostile excitement generated in South Asia by evolutionary theory. In fact, though, the modern Hindu ideology in the style of Vivekananda and Radhakrishnan did not take evolutionism very seriously: that was left to Sri Aurobindo, who took up one of the spiritual options, namely seeing evolution as itself a mental and spiritual unfolding of the divine (in this Aurobindo is the Hindu counterpart of Teilhard de Chardin). (c) Further, the Neo-Advaitin doctrine of the unity of all religions could be regarded as drawing upon an important theme in Indianness since way back, the unity behind the manifestations of the divine, and could at the same time function as an effective riposte to Christian evangelicalism: *Et tu, Christe*. All religions point to the same truth, but Hindu Advaita has a certain superiority, for it has known this all along, the monotheisms having at best wavered in their generosity to other faiths. (d) This inclusiveness helped to deal effectively both with the growth of nationalism and the challenge of Western democratic forms. Inclusiveness could provide a Hindu basis for Indian unity: Muslims, Jains, agnostics, Buddhists, Christians and Parsees could all be offered a stake in the emerging Indian national consciousness. (e) At the same time inclusiveness could serve to define a special Indian doctrine of the secular State. The secular State would not meant that India is not religious. It would mean separation of religion and State, since all religions would have an equal claim before the law (save for one or two elements such as cow-protection, as it turned out). There are, be it noted, two quite different and unrelated ideas of secularity: Church-state separation and non-religiousness. In any case the new Hindu ideology was irenic, often unrealistically so. A less theologically formed version of the same theme was put forward by Mahatma Gandhi, with his concept of Truth as supreme spiritual and ethical value. (f) The modern Hindu ideology also was worked out at the interface between traditional and Western culture and education by the happy confluence between the traditional saintly teacher Ramakrishna and the Western educated cosmopolitan Vivekananda. Incidentally the Indo-Western combination of Gandhi and Nehru was much less effective in the long run because of a deep rift between the thinking of the two: Gandhi's rejection of industrial capitalism and Nehru's sceptism about Hindu spirituality made problems for the future of Congress after Independence.

The new ideology, then, helped to cope with and *assimilate relevant elements of the intruding worldviews* and politico-religious themes. At the same time it left *intact* most of the Hindu tradition, but in a modernizable form. I shall not go through my list to demonstrate this. At the same time it injected some Christian themes into the Hindu experience: a call for social action and moral reform, and the use of missionary methods. All this could be geared both to the rediscovery of Indianness but also to the national struggle. Like other forms of chauvinist nationalism, British imperialism had rationalized its expansion by appealing to doctrines of civilized democratic and Christian values: these could be appealed to and turned around by Indian nationalists. To do so, though, Hindu society itself needed criticism, and this could be fostered through the acceptance of the positive elements of Western-style education.

Through all of this a new conception of Hinduism, rooted however in the ancient past, was created. There were resources there to be developed and exploited in the new situation of the White Frontier. The contrast with Sri Lanka is instructive. Although the revival of Buddhism in a modern setting in Ceylon was connected with the work of the Theosophical Society (itself an interesting and syncretic new religion, with universalizing tendencies), the *Buddhist tradition did not have the relevant shape to produce the required synthesis*. The reasons were largely these:

First, Theravada Buddhism, in lacking the notion of a divine Being behind the whole cosmos, cannot produce an ideology of unity behind diverse representations of the divine. Buddhism is in many ways a highly tolerant religion, but it has its special slant on the world. Hinduism has better resources for the unity-of-religions move. Second, Buddhism had come to be identified with a particular linguistic and cultural group, namely the Sinhala. The various narratives of the chronicles of Sri Lanka, ranging from the Mahavamsa of the 5th century C.E. to those of the 13th, 14th, and 18th centuries, celebrated the Buddhist character of the people. The religion was associated with struggles to preserve and expand Sinhala identity. On the other hand the struggle towards independence was not as difficult as in the case of India, and the transition to independence was rather serene. Thus though there were Sinhala grievances against the British, they were not so bitter as easily to generate a violent or deeply felt countervailing nationalist resurgence. That was characteristically delayed till nearly a decade after independence, with the formation of the Sri Lanka Freedom Party administration. But the use of Buddhist resources from the past to foster national identity was necessarily divisive, in the Sri Lankan contest, because of the importance of the Tamil and other minorities: especially the longstanding Tamil presence. Thus Sri Lanka has become deeply divided on religious and communal lines, in which that characteristic modern phenomenon, the blending of religion and nationalism, has on both sides brewed up the recent terrible storms in the island.

This illustrates a general point about changes across the White Frontier: what happens in part depends upon the shape of the religious and cultural resources on the other side of that frontier. Hinduism was well fitted to provide an indigenous resource for struggle against the British. Of course the configuration of the Frontier was important also: thus India and Ceylon had the advantage (in a sense) of being conquered and given a kind of unity through the occupying institutions. By contrast China was disrupted from the outside, and the transactions across the Frontier were more disturbing and chaotic. (But we could note also that the Chinese tradition was less suited for various reasons to respond to the pressures of modernizing, and the very strength of traditional education proved a weakness, when the Confucian literary mode was inadequate to the challenges of a changing industrial and scientific world).

The new Hindu ideology was a classical, not a primoridalist or post-primordialist synthesis. It can be said to be a form of neo-classicism, but also a syncretism with intruder themes. It was also selective: other forms of Vedanta for instance were less suited to the total syntheis. They could be attractive, it is true. Tagore's presentation of a Westernized version of the *acintyabhedābheda* of the Vaisnava goswamis is a case in point. It was a reshaped Advaita that promised best for the recreation of Hindu identity, and this accounts for its remarkable success among educated and spiritually minded Hindus.

If we may loosely assign the term fundamentalist to those movements which go back to origins, and near-origins to represent the faith in a supposedly purified form (but usually one incorporating a blend with other modern and often intruding motifs), then the Arya Samaj, and for that matter the Brahmo Samajis, can be seen as fundamentalists: but the Neo-Vedanta is neo-classical. It is also neo-traditional. It is worth commenting that true traditionalism merely ignores the White Frontier and carries on. Increasingly such deep traditionalism has become difficult, because of the intrusive character of the White Frontier.

Incidentally, when an ethnic faith and culture (of which Hinduism can be counted a complex example) encounters a universalist challenge – as represented by Christianity and Western culture, often blended in a powerful though rather unstable hybrid – then it needs somehow to hit back with its own universalism. This can most naturally be done by appeal to some kind of federal ideal: that is, by considering that one's own people needs to express its adherence to a universal spirituality in its own particular way. Another alternative is to represent one's own cultural adaptation of the intruding faith as being the true interpretation (but this presupposes giving up much of the content of one's own tradition).

There is another factor in the dynamics of interchange across the Frontier which I have not mentioned: it is the existence of the socialist and especially the Marxist tradition, both Western and anti-traditional, and both modern and anti-capitalist. Because the operations of capitalism are not in a colonialist environment perceived, even by many in the new bourgeoisie, as benign, socialism as anti-capitalism has its attractions; but it can represent too traumatic a way of asserting a new life, since at least in its Marxist form it will generate an assault on indigenous as well as on intruding forms of religion. It is though, possible to experiment with various moderate compromises, such as Buddhist socialism, Islamic socialism and so on.

To sum up: various possibilities of change occur where lies the White Frontier, and more generally where any cultural boundary lies. What happens is in part dependent on the shape of the existing tradition. If for the sake of simplicity we refer to the two aspects of White culture as being Christianity and modernism, each aspect of course sub-dividing into Catholic and Protestant, liberal and socialist, and so on, then reactions to intrusion can take the form of a kind of ostrich traditionalism, or neo-traditionalism in which classical religion reinterpreted is blended with modernism, or blended too with some minor elements of Christianity, or a sort of fundamentalism blended with modernity.

Or again one can attempt to take an antiforeign stance through a Marxism, combining that with a non-religious affirmation of the values of the culture. Various other possibilities and combinations present themselves. One of these is to reject crucial aspects of modernism and yet to accept Christianity, or major elements thereof, into the fabric of traditional faith. This is the Gandhian approach.

I now wish to comment on what lies on the Western side of the Frontier, and to consider the degree to which it is possible for various elements within the Indian tradition to be taken up independently of the traditional collages. I present the following brief thoughts on my list, giving the ways in which the themes in question have their own special existence beyond the Hindu, Buddhist, etc., heritage.

(1) *Bhakti*: probably the most striking export of this mode of life is through Hare Krishna. But here we are dealing with the adaptation of a subtradition. The movement thus takes on the characteristics of a sect. (2) The *yoga* mode: indeed an array of forms of yogic meditation often synthesized and simplified into an ecumenical yoga has become widespread in the West and elsewhere. (3) and (4) *Rebirth* and *Karma*: these ideas have some attraction in the West, and are sometimes hitched onto non-oriental worldviews. (5) *Holy men*: modern communications and travel have given new life to the figure of the wandering holy person, often functioning as guru. Here is a case of new dynamics emerging as the guru crosses the Frontier; but also within India itself there emerges the possibility of the new non-regional guru who can appeal to the educated middle class (e.g. Sai Baba). (6) *Monasticism*: It may be noted that monasticism does not have that relatively freewheeling role that the individual guru can perform, so that both in the case of Buddhist monasticism and for such as the Ramakrishna Vedanta movement the modern milieu means a reinforcement of the embedding of monasticism in a tradition and a wider organization. (7) and (8) Ideas of *liberation* and *dharma*: It may be noted that with the emergence of these ideas into a wider world context, they can be presented essentially as detached from the particularities of Indian culture, much as salvation and ethics as possibilities are seen within Western evangelism. (9) The mass of *mythic* material can now function as a kind of

psychological resource, so that Hindu and certain aspects of Mahayana and Vajrayana myth particularly can come to form dreamlike material prized for its depth–psychological meaning; consider in this the writings of Jung, Eliade and Wendy O'Flaherty; (10) and somewhat similarly with the way Eastern *art* can be taken up. (11) and (12): The *scriptural* traditions, both within India and outside, now have become, by translation and book production, a private spiritual resource, no longer imprisoned as it were by the restrictions on knowledge imposed by traditional society. In other words, the scriptures have gone from *śruti* to anthology. (13) The traditional *philosophical* learning also has undergone transformation in India, and in some respects has entered world culture: moreover the history of Indian thought has now been given a narrative through the work of such writers as Dasgupta and Radhakrishnan. (14) The *guru*: see above under 5. (15) *Ethics* in the cosmos: see 8 above. (16) The *cosmos*: both among Hindus and in Buddhism there is satisfaction that the scale of traditional cosmology has some congruence with modern science. (17) Sacramental *rituals*: the dynamics of modernity tend to shift attention away from ritualism, and thus rituals tends to subordinate themselves to the pursuit of higher mental states (consider the wide role of the mantra in modern guru-oriented cults). It is important to note too that in the ever more significant Hindu diaspora in such areas as Fiji, Guyana, Mauritius, Natal and England, it is less easy to maintain the old ritual fabric, and more doctrinally and experientially oriented movements have a more vital role to play (also the household rites diminish with the almost inevitable decay of the extended family). (18) Household rites: see 17. (19) *Purity* and *impurity* and (20) the *cow* make sense largely within the fabric of India itself: but they are as it happens in some tension with modernity and social reform. (21) Astrology: this can be made technical and get detached from its full South Asian milieu, merging with Western astrology in new syntheses. (22) The *hierarchical* mode of society: this is scarcely capable of export or meaning outside the dense fabric of Indian life itself. (23) *Austerities*: These appear to have diminished in importance, partly because creative power has been psychologized somewhat and with it the power of *tapas*. But we may note that Gandhi imparted a new social meaning to renunciation. This is where we see an older resource being taken up and given a new function and power within anovel milieu. (24) Though for much of the West pilgrimage has now become tourism, in traditional societies new technologies of transport have profoundly affected the dynamics of pilgrimage: thus it can have a more unifying effect than in the past (e.g. Kataragama has become a pan-Sri-Lankan deity and place of pilgrimage). (25), (26) and (27) Various ideas of divine unity, pluralism and theologies: these have been taken up in a new global context, no longer as a specifically Hindu phenomenon but as a theory of global unity.

All this may be summed up by saying that when intruding forces arrive they impart a new dynamic to the elements of the tradition, and conversely when elements of the tradition travel into a different milieu, likewise changes occur. And this is part of a more general structural observation that thematic elements affect one another by juxtaposition and integration into collages. One of the continual fascinations of Indianness is the way we can see so many possibilities realized. So: can you have yoga without bhakti? Yes. And the pair combined so that yoga is seen as a form of devotion or devotion is seen as a means of self-training? Why yes. Can you have yoga with great tapas? Yes. And without it? Yes. Can you have bhakti with icons? Of course. Without them? That too. Can you have yoga with ritual? Yes. And without it? Yes. Can you have bhakti with scriptures? Yes. Without them? That too. Can pilgrimage aim at a guru? Yes. And not? Yes. So we go on. So many combinations of possibilities can be realized.

But the same treatment turns out to be possible for Christianity and other religions. Priests, hierarchies, pastors, sacramental ritual, preaching, extensive doctrine, the cult of saints, scriptural authority, prophetic experience, mysticism, conversion: we can see ways in which these elementary themes can be combined and sundered. And we can see too that across the Frontier of modernity these themes change: consider the profound change which modern communications have effected on the Papacy. The strength of John Paul II is that he seized an implicit possibility and developed it.

And that seems to me how the history of the human spirit often works – combining and recombining the themes and possibilities in new collages which attempt to satisfy the multiple and deep interests of human beings and to call upon the profound resources which the traditions make available. If I have emphasized modernism in this discussion it is partly because it is so potent a stimulus of religious and other change, and partly because it helps us to see that religious and non-religious themes and worldviews have to be taken together. Hence I believe that the new incarnation of the comparative study of religion has to be *cross-cultural dynamic worldview analysis*.

7

The Future of Religions

Probably the most fruitful way of trying to predict the future of religion is through what may be called dynamic worldview analysis. Thus it is wise to consider religions as a species of the genus worldviews which also includes ideologies. That is, though our own Western society makes a distinction between religions and secular belief-systems, the distinction itself is an ideological or religious one and is unscientific in failing to see how functionally over the wide range of dimensions religions and secular ideologies function similarly. By 'dynamic' I have in mind two things: first how worldviews often combine synergistically, as in religious nationalism; and second how worldviews develop dynamically in interaction both with others and with other forces. Thus we may study the combinations and interactions of worldviews. These seem to follow certain patterns.

The word 'worldviews' has certain disadvantages, perhaps sounding too disembodied and cerebral. But there seems to be no other equally suitable word in English, to cover, as I have said, both secular and traditionally religious belief and practice systems. I would like to correct the impression created by the word by noting that worldviews tend to have six chief dimensions – not only doctrine, myth (or loaded narrative), and ethics, but also ritual, experience (feeling) and social (institutional) embodiment.

To predict the future it is necessary to rely upon some generalizations arising from looking at the recent or more distant past. But there are obviously many imponderables even about this. While the scientific study of religion, in a broad sense, is quite well developed in certain Western countries, notably the United States and Canada, it tends to be employed reflexively on those societies and less intensively upon others. Further, about worldview data we are woefully ignorant when it comes to recent China and large areas of the Marxist world, and for differing reasons in other areas such as Latin America. So we need guesswork even in describing the immediate past over large areas of the world.

Clearly also it is not unimportant that different religions and religious movements, and differing ideologies, have differing characteristics. Marxism becomes more rapidly and centrally institutionalized than scientific humanism; Protestantism is more individualistic than Islam; Buddhism has a very different attitude to gods and God than most other religions; and so on. Thus, we need to pay attention to the internal dynamics of the various worldviews, and to the effect on these of interactions.

It is useful to start with an overview of the religious and ideological state of the world. It is, of course, an obvious fact about modern life that the world itself is in an intensely interactive condition: jet planes, transnational corporations, electronic communications, movements of people, the threat of global war – these and other phenomena help to bind the globe into a more tightly knit whole. But against this as a counterpoint there are also regional divergences resulting from differences of history, geography, economics and political relations. Let me briefly describe the main seven blocs into which the world has arranged itself.

First there are those countries forming, roughly speaking, the democratic West: West European countries, Scandinavia, the United States, Canada, Australia, New Zealand and one or two smaller offshoots. These countries have a largely Christian background, practice various forms of social democracy and are by the same token capitalist, though with a modification of the system. Increasingly there is an admixture of non-Christian religious and cultural groups, as well as a strong strand of scientific humanism and intuitive agnosticism. Thus religiously and culturally such countries are increasingly pluralistic: indeed some Asian and other beliefs and practices are making some headway among the indigenous traditionally Christian population.

Second, there is the bloc of countries under various versions of Marxist rule, from East Germany to North Korea. Here in some respects the Marxist ideologies function somewhat like official religions – Party-State alliance substituting for Church-State solidarity. Generally traditional religions have fared badly. Islam and Christianity have been suppressed in Albania, Buddhism for a long period in China and Tibet, Christianity purged and repressed in the USSR and elsewhere – and so on. Buddhism especially has fared disastrously in most of the Marxist countries of Asia. On the other hand Catholicism in Poland and Orthodoxy in Romania flourish and are tolerated guardedly by the regimes.

Third, there is the Islamic crescent ranging from Indonesia to West Africa, through Malaysia, Bangladesh, Pakistan, the Middle East, North Africa and so on. In many areas a backlash against Western corrupting influences (for so they are often perceived) is evident. Islam is becoming more ecumenical at the same time, in that the aeroplane has made the pilgrimage to Mecca easier and in other ways modern conditions give easier scope for mutuality in the Islamic world. But there is a continuing crisis as to how Islamic values should be accommodated to modernity: hence experiments like Khomeini's Shi'i nationalism, Ghaddafi's Islamic socialism, the Islamic constitutions of Pakistan, the Sudan and Malaysia, the activities of the Muslim Brotherhood in Syria, Egypt and elsewhere, etc.

Fourth, there are the predominantly non-Islamic, non-Marxist cultures of old Asia: those of the Indian sub-continent (India, Sri Lanka, Nepal, Bhutan), of South East Asia (Burma, Thailand, Singapore), and of East Asia (Taiwan, South Korea, Japan). Here various mixtures of Hinduism, Buddhism and Confucianism traditionally have predominated. As a result of events since World War II, these countries have mixed forms of capitalism with traditional cultures, and mostly have democratic attributes (but Burma has kept out Western and capitalist influences to a great degree; while Taiwan has an authoritarian regime as also increasingly Singapore). The economic success of the East Asian countries and the pluralism of the South Asian countries have introduced a secular perspective and yet religion has also had freedom to develop without repression.

Fifth, there is Latin America, from Santa Barbara California to Patagonia, plus the Caribbean: a world mostly influenced religiously by Catholicism, but containing other traditional elements, and often sceptical of the beneficence of northern capitalism: here there is an increasing alienation of the Catholic Church from government and also vigour among Protestant missionary groups, especially among tribal peoples.

Sixth, Black Africa south of the Sahara shows great religious vitality. Though traditional African religion is on the defensive and Christianity is the predominant religion (though in many areas Islam is also important), new forms of African faith are vigorous: mostly they are black movements combining traditional motifs or structures and Christian themes. Such black independent churches number over ten thousand, and three thousand of these are to be found in South Africa. Some are relatively largescale and mainstream such as the Kimbanguists of Zaire. Many are small; but they represent new ways of interpreting African religious experience. Marxism and African forms of socialism are also important: such as Nyerere's rural socialism in Tanzania, the new radicalism of Ethiopia, and socialist gradualism in Zimbabwe. Furthermore, there is in South Africa an important religious and ideological struggle between whites (and Afrikaaner Christian nationalism in particular) and varieties of black and Asian groups.

Seventh, there are the many smaller countries of the Pacific. Missionary Christianity has largely replaced older Polynesian, Melanesian and other religions; on the whole politically these lands are deeply influenced by Western forms of social democracy; and at the same time have to cope with the large economic forces which play upon them from the capitalist North.

How, then, will these varied segments of world culture evolve religiously? There are two major, and opposing forces, which need to be taken into account to answer this question, and which will have their effects in differing ways in all these cultural areas. One is nationalism and the other individualism. For it is a notable fact of the last 200 years of world history, from about the time of the French Revolution, that increasingly power has been redistributed to sovereign nation-states; first in Europe, then in the colonial world. Now virtually all the land of the Earth is divided into national entities. Often national identity is provided by religion or secular worldview: Poland by Catholicism, Burma by Buddhism, China by Maoism, East Germany by Marxism, etc. Religious resurgence can be connected often to a combination of traditional values and modern nationalist revival. On the other hand, various political and economic developments in modern times have converged to make individualism a powerful solvent of collective loyalties and traditional ties: the liberal humanism of the Enlightenment combined with capitalism, and modern forms of production. Oddly even in collectivist countries, a certain privatisation of the individual's deeper choices – as to worldview and as to personal relationships – has occurred.

Given then these various blocs and forces in place, what predictions can we make about the future of religion and other ideologies over the next thirty to fifty years? Let us begin with Christianity – or rather to be more realistic, Christianities. The main stream of Protestantism in many countries has made an accommodation with liberal humanism, and a similar blending is visible in the results of Vatican II (1962–65). This has generated an ecumenical Christianity in the Northern countries; but the future sees increasingly the centre of gravity of Christianities as moving South, for while Christianity flourishes in varied forms in black Africa and has a new dynamism born of liberation theology in the Latin American region, ecumenical Christianity in the North will probably continue to diminish statistically, because societies as they become more pluralist and individualist relax pressures towards standard options in faith. So we can predict that more and more ecumenical leaders will be drawn from the South. The role of Christianities in national life will be less pronounced, except somewhat politically. For it is an obvious consequence of a Southerly direction in Christianity that it should become more critical of wealthier societies. So the Christianities of an ecumenical kind will draw increasingly upon crosscultural sources of criticism. The majority of Christians moreover will be in the South.

But ecumenical Christianity will, as itself a blend, be matched by a reaction. Ecumenical Christianity will not necessarily speak to the condition of those in Northern society who need reassurance about identity and community. A continued growth in patriotic evangelical Christianity will be notable, and this will have effects in the mission field, for this sort of religion can make inroads in traditional religious and tribal areas outside the main stream of the ecumenical type of Christianity – e.g. in the Latin South, in Africa and in India and East Asia. It will also have an impact in the Marxisms, where it can get a foothold, for it can appeal to those who are alienated from the ecumenical, accommodating Christianity in such countries as Romania and the Soviet Union. Here it must be remembered that this 'backlash' Christianity has pioneered electronic evangelization in the United States, and it is possible to use the media to jump walls: obviously much more so in the next fifty years.

I have assumed in the above remarks that Protestant ecumenical Christianities and the Papacy will be in harmony. One of the reasons is that the forces of *aggiornamento* unleashed by Pope John XXIII are impossible to halt: and in a plural and mobile world Catholics will increasingly recognize their choice, and that they as individuals do not need to heed the dictates of the Papacy (this has already happened in the Western countries in regard to birth control, where the great majority of Catholics fail to practice what the Pope preaches). Thus a more eclectic Catholicism will find itself in harmony more and more with liberal Protestantism. Whether any formal alliance or merger between Catholics and others occurs is not all that important. Ecumenical Christianity will be a kind of polymorphous transnational spiritual movement, with its strengths lying in two directions – its encouragement of private spirituality (which is where alliances with the East are attractive) and of a social critique of global injustice.

Intellectually the Marxisms will continue to be in crisis; and also in a sense spiritually. Thus it is likely that the religious alternative will come more openly to the surface: Buddhism in China, Orthodoxy in Russia, Islam in Central Asia. In the new conditions however the accent is likely to be on personal mystical religion than on highly ritualized external forms. Therefore certain forms of Buddhism and Islam, for instance, are more likely to achieve prominence – Ch'an and Sufism, for instance (already Sufism plays a vital role in maintaining the vigour of Islam in Central Asia: you can close mosques, but not an inner quest).

Adjacent to Christianity and now overwhelmingly represented in Western countries plus Israel is Judaism. We note here too a backlash to moderate forms of Judaism (e.g. Conservative and Reform Judaism). The Hasidic revival and a new fundamentalist Orthodox Judaism have political undertones of varying kinds. Obviously the future of Judaism depends much on events in Israel: but if in fact there is a general settlement in the Middle East we may see a further secularization of the population, already predominantly non-practising. The alliance between Synagogue and State already causes resentment among many Israeli Jews. In any case the centre of gravity of Jewish civilization will remain in the United States. Because there is a problem there of the retention of Jewish identity, it is likely that conservative interpretations of Jewish teaching will grow, and that paradoxically the practice of Judaism in Israel will decline as it intensifies in the United States.

The third great Western monotheism, Islam, has a future full of turbulence: for it has special problems in adapting to the new global order. First, there is likely to continue to develop a politico-religious struggle, spearheaded by so-called 'fundamentalist' Muslims, whether Shi'i or Sunni, represented now most clearly by Iranian radicalism and the Muslim Brotherhood respectively. Since such revived Islam is very strong among students across the Islamic world, it has a powerful future, as new generations of revolutionaries are nurtured. Especially prone to upheaval are countries which have absorbed much Western influence, such as Egypt and Tunisia, as well as Syria and Iraq. Islamic self-consciousness will also become assertive in the Republic of India, which is the third largest Muslim country in the world. It is likely that anti-modernist revolutions will occur in a central swathe of Arab countries, and that further warfare between India and its Muslim neighbours will develop in the Subcontinent. It is likely indeed that most of the Islamic crescent will turn to relatively anti-Western, and anti-Marxist, attitudes over the next twenty years or more. This will affect Muslim minorities in South Africa, Guyana and elsewhere, including Britian and North America. But second, Islam will increasingly see itself as a global minority. It has never been happy with a minority position, having to conform to outer norms. This will reinforce its unease about identity: and the new Islamic radicalism will have an ecumenical character, despite the historic split between Shi'i and Sunni traditions. This, incidentally, may pose a greater threat to the Soviet Union than the West, since revivalist Islam is content to trade; but is and will be impatient of foreign dominance of historically Islamic areas, such as Central Asia. (Whether a Middle East settlement can survive renascent Islamic radicalism is questionable, incidentally.)

From the point of view of dynamic worldview analysis, the Islamic predicament can be looked on as the interaction between Islamic tradition and two great ideological segments, Western individualist humanism on the one hand and modern science, technology and economics on the other. Islamic modernism represents a synthesis of all three, as for instance in much middle class Egyptian Islam. Turkey rejected the Islamic tradition in its revolution and tried to cultivate the two segments. Khomeini and other revivalists wish to have the tradition (reformed) plus the scientific, technological and economic segment (with minimal adaptations). But can one have modernity without individualism?

That is the agonizing question of many traditional societies wishing to conserve tradition and at the same time modernize. The same problem afflicts Deng's China: can we conserve Marxist tradition and have modern technology without corrosive individualism?

Turning now to Hinduism, mainly in India, but present in a not insignificant diaspora, what of the future there? The Hindu ethos happens to be very open to modern science and a pluralistic society. Its modern exponents have provided a synthesis which sees religion and science as revealing differing aspects of the one universe. Much of modernist religion in the West has moved in the same direction. But for the future Hinduism is likely to move in new social directions. Its major problem remains caste and untouchability. Also, the older Hindu claim that all religions can live together as pointing to the same Truth will not easily cope with the resurgence of Islam. The time is ripe on the first front for a renewal of Hindu–Marxist synthesis – a kind of 'liberation theology' in the Hindu context. Unfortunately although India with its open society and plural attitudes is well suited to make the best of Western science in the next thirty years, this may increase the gap between the middle class and the poor, especially the untouchables. The latter have in the past experimented with converting to Christianity, and in the period up to World War II Buddhism, under the leadership of Dr. Ambedkar: the next logical move is to move towards Islam, already powerful in Indian society. This will produce a deep crisis in India, and quite possibly civil war, with intervention maybe from Islamic countries.

Buddhism has a different future. First, it will continue to grow in the West, where it is already well rooted in Europe and the US especially. It is an attractive alternative to theism, and in some ways complementary to Christianity. Second, there is a chance, as we have already noted, for a revival of individualistic Buddhism in the Marxist countries, especially China. Third, in the independent Buddhist countries of South and South-East Asia it will continue to be identified with nationalism. Fourth, there are small signs of its gaining a foothold in Africa, and though it will never perhaps capture the African mind to the degree Christianity has, it will doubtless make its presence felt. So worldwide there will be increased consciousness of Buddhism as a universal religion and philosophy, very consonant with modern science (the doctrine of impermanence for instance reduces the universe to a flux of short-lived microscopic events). In a world with rising educational attainments it will increase its appeal. Moreoever, for various reasons it can live in friendly competition with Christianity, and the religions will influence one another, no doubt, profoundly: arriving maybe at a synthesis which can provide an East–West *rapprochement* in the context of liberal humanist thought. This East-West interplay has already been important in Japan's economic development, and may herald a new revival of Buddhist thought in Japan after a period of some intellectual lethargy.

The role of Eastern religions in Western society raises also the question of whether a 'world faith' is possible. But it is obvious that the dynamics of our present condition point towards reactions as well as syntheses. Moreover the logic of the segments of individualism and Western scientific modernity is towards a plural existence. But there may emerge a viewpoint which will have great attraction over a wide area. For it is not only the West that is interested in pluralistic societies. In the Southern world we are faced with a large number of relatively small-scale cultures, mostly influenced as we have seen by Christianity. The search for identity implies a sort of cultural and spiritual federalism. The proliferation of new religions in this Southern world and in small-scale societies everywhere is all about the retaining of something from the spiritually vital past in a new context. So both West, Old Asia and the South have an interest in a kind of pluralistic federation of the spirit serving as an umbrella for the variegated search for identity and a deeper life. In a way Los Angeles (for all its faults) is a foretaste of this pluralism; many of the ethnicities of the South, cultures of the East and varieties of the West live together in a federation of quarters and districts. So it may be that something like a new Pacific mind will emerge in which the interplay of East, West and South will provide a pluralistic search for the ultimate.

Meanwhile both the West and Africa and elsewhere will continue no doubt to bubble with new religious movements. One can predict that their numbers will multiply, because in a 'shrunk globe' the number of cultural interfaces will have grown in number to cover virtually all possibilities of mutual interaction (as also in the artistic, culinary, musical and other contexts).

Many composite worldviews stay in individuals' heads, but others take off. It is hard to predict which will: would you think that Evangelical Confucianism (with ingredients also of technological modernity and anti-communism as a form of ecumenical patriotism) would take off? It did: it is the Unification Church of the Reverend Moon. Each merger is not just of course a mechanical blend but can involve creative particularities. Who would expect the Hellenized Pharisaism centering upon a messianic prophet would take off in the Roman Empire? It did: its name now is Christianity. So there are some limits to our knowing which of present spiritual and ideological movements will 'take off' into our global future. But there is no reason to suppose that the present great religions will always be the only ones.

Finally let me say something about how we may foresee the traditional religions evolving, in regard to their dimensions. For one can perceive certain shifts which will continue into the future. First, there is a tendency for complex and everyday ritual to be eroded by modernization. For one thing annual calendrical cycles were appropriate to older pre-technological agriculture. For another thing increasingly mobile populations, even in poor countries, drift out of the more staid ritual setting of a settled milieu. Again, in so far as much ritual in everyday life has a magical function, it gets superseded by technical processes. In Marxist states public rituals can be abolished or deeply restricted. In more individualistic versions of secular society ritual becomes privatized and made informal.

But this does not mean that the expressive side of ritual is without significance. For inner attitudes and feelings come to be more strongly expressed as outer ritual fades. Once, for instance, being 'born again' was a metaphor for the sacrament of baptism. But it also acquires a psychological, inner-spiritual meaning: a Christian's experience of feeling saved. So we may continue in the future to see much more emphasis on the experiential than on the ritual dimension of religion, both because of the privatization of religion under the pressures of Marxist government and because of the individualism of capitalist societies. Moreover, the same forces that generate the individual search within also help to transform authoritative institutions into voluntary ones. In the West and in many parts of the South, we can expect religious authority to be considerably weakened and a more pluralistic stance adopted. Here certain aspects of the religious traditions can get emphasized rather than others: yoga and mystical experience in the ambit of Hinduism and beyond; Sufi mysticism in Islamic contexts; the Kabbalah in the Jewish tradition; aesthetic appreciation and existential attitudes in the ambience of scientific humanism; and so on. We may dub this a kind of religious romanticism: looking towards the non-rational, experiential rapport with cosmic realities as they are perceived by individuals. And it fits with trends of doctrine and philosophy, since mainstream Christianity, Buddhism, Hindusim and Islam are not overmuch troubled by the supposed warfare between science and religion (myths of creation and so on are no longer taken literally by most adherents of modern Protestantism and Catholicism – leaving aside the more radical conservatives). There is thus emerging a new monism in which religion and science play complementary roles in our understanding and responding to the universe. We can thus see a kind of 'romantic monism' as a major trend in the religious thinking of the future. But again there are backlashes to consider: reaffirmations of hardline interpretations of scripture, and so on. It is likely that the romantic monism I have sketched will sit somewhat lightly to sacred narrative. Thus the details of Biblical narrative will be less important than the general impression of Christ's presence (for the Christian) or of ethical teachings. So both myth and ritual in their present forms are likely to be less important than in the past. Because of this religions will prove less exclusive, for it is easier to agree or at least to converge in regard to experience and ethics than upon ritual and myth. But it should be emphasized that these remarks have to be seen in the light of vigorous reactive movements, across the face of Islam, among Jews in search of identity, among evangelical Christians, dogmatic Marxists and so on. I may also add that the monism of doctrine goes well with social pluralism.

These then are some foreseeable trends in religion. The probable changes which have the most powerful meaning politically are these: the convergence of the interests of Christianity and Western humanism on the one hand, and Buddhism and other religions on the other; and their joint relevance both to democratic pluralism and the ethnic pluralism of the South; the ecumenical North-South character emerging in Christianity which will make the Churches more critical of the present economic system; the emergence of much privatized religion in the Marxist countries; and the wider spread of Islamic radicalism, in conflict both with Western and Marxist values. Finally, there is the likelihood that the number of new religious movements will greatly increase in the interactive cultural setting of our large cities where ethnic groups from all parts of the world are in contact. As for these new movements: some no doubt will grow into great forces, but it is hard to predict which, since it is difficult to estimate how deep symbolisms will stir wide human response. It is certain of course that the present large traditions will continue, and many well entrenched smaller faiths, such as Sikhism, Jainism, Mormonism and so on. Scientific humanism as a worldview will also have a strong impact on non-Western cultures. So we shall see a continuing debate within the streets of the global city as to the right ethical, spiritual and political stances suitable to humankind's ultimate welfare.

If my analysis is correct it points to areas of danger. Not only are advances in unity accompanied by hardline backlash phenomena, but the difficult relations between Christianity, Islam, Judaism and Marxism and the friction between radical Hindu and Islamic values could be major factors in warfare over the next thirty years.

8

A Global Ethic Arising from the Epistemology of Religious and Similar Value-Systems

Since the time of the Enlightenment we in the West have got used to the idea of the autonomy of morals, yet of course this very idea could be thought to depend upon a worldview of a certain sort. On the other hand not only are there behavioural requirements which must be observed on the whole if society is not to break down, but also behind them are typical ideal attitudes (love towards all, compassion, a sense of brotherhood, the golden rule) which are found widely expressed in world literature and social teachings. All this justifies us in speaking of a 'moral strand' which is a component of religious and other worldviews. But, and this is the point of my remark about the autonomy of morals, the moral strand is woven differently into the fabrics of differing worldviews and is variously affected by them. Sometimes, for instance, what in the West count as moral commands are embedded in a system of divine or sacred law; sometimes the right is what is commanded by God; sometimes good behaviour is seen as conformity with a cosmic pattern, such as the Tao or the Dharma; and sometimes moral rules are justified by a secularly stated utilitarianism; and so on. It is thus a useful model to think of a moral ingredient consisting of a relatively stable set of ideas, precepts and attitudes which both affects and is affected by the worldview contexts of the varied traditions and subtraditions. I want to discuss some implications of this model for the possibility of a global ethic. I shall argue that the model implies a soft non-relativism which in turn implies certain values: in brief that a higher-order situation has lower-order implications. I shall also consider what the presuppositions are not just of the over-lappingly plural character of ethical systems as we find them in the world, but also of our very study. The comparative or corsscultural study of religions and worldviews, if conducted in a descriptive and critical manner, yields values which may be in conflict with the methods and attitudes of lower-order systems. Thus: taking seriously some beliefs, such as those of the Bahai, may conflict with the zeal and religious epistemology of many Muslims. Where scripture or learned authority is committed to some thesis in the history of religions it is liable to collide with the findings of modern studies in the field. Sometimes these collisions are profound, and open up to us some deep issues about the very possibility of a global ethics.

It may be useful, before coming directly to these points to look at some of the major alternative worldvews in the world today. Such a sketch enables to bear in mind the actualities with which any global ethics proposals have to deal. To try to categorize the lifeways of a myriad societies is foolhardy: but it may have some virtue in the focusing of our thought. Many of these outlooks and moral systems are in fact syncretisms, to complicate matters: syncretisms between secular ideologies or ideological themes, such as liberalism and nationalism, and traditional beliefs, or between Marxist socialism and nationalism, and so on. Generally, because of this, traditions as they emerge into today's world, take differing forms – as premodern ways of life persisting obliviously into the present time; as tradition mixed with liberalism and modernity; as reactive tradition – neoconservatism, mingling, typically, technological modernity, a reinterpreted tradition (neo-foundational, or neoclassical, etc., often lumped together as 'fun-damentalist') often having nationalist overtones. Thus the SLFP variety of Buddhism in Sri Lanka tends to be neoclassical rein-terpreted Theravada Buddhism, shown to be compatible with scientific modernity, and nationalist in tone. The moral majority is a similar Protestant movement, but neofoundational and yet rejecting modernity in relation to historical scholarship but not in regard to technology, and likewise nationalistic. By contrast ecumenical Christianity tends to be liberal and internationalist. To complicate matters it is possible to take different stances, or blends thereof, in regard to the differing dimensions of religion: being perhaps institutionally traditionalist, ritually modernistic, doctrinally neofoundationalist, ethically liberal, experientially syncretic and mythically modernistic – consider a modern Catholic, defending and maintaining the ecclesiastical institutions rather conservatively, reaffirming the first creeds, taking a progressive line in moral teachings, absorbing the pentecostalist tradition of ecstatic experience into Church life, and reading salvation history in secularist terms. All these complications of the emerging forms of traditions are laid on top of the various layers of regional and denominational variegation of the past as transmitted to us.

So doubly do we have an obligation to speak of Christianities, Islams and so on in the plural. For all their plural character, perhaps because of it, the religious traditions retain great power, but alongside and blending with some major ideological traditions and motifs: liberal humanism (or humanisms), Marxism, and nationalism. Some traditions, having lost their main habitat, such as Confucianism, are perhaps most important as resources for humankind to draw upon: in general of course we live in a syncretic, pragmatic age in which a novel eclecticism is possible. A special problem is seen among relatively small-scale traditions, those particularly that are identified with particular ethnic or tribal cultures chiefly in the Third World. They have to make adaptation to the powerful incoming forces of Christianity (and Islam), modernity, liberalism, etc., but typically without a strong enough classical indigenous base. One solution is to move towards a more universal regionalism – hence such concepts as African religion and Native American religion have been created; another solution is to move towards a federal theory of religions – that each has something to offer within the wider whole. Thus tradition can be maintained, no doubt with modifications, and at the same time one's spiritual heritage becomes a *resource* for humanity. An example is how Native American attitudes and concepts are used to reinforce a universal environmentalism.

This leads to the thought that one consequence of mutual awareness of cultures will be a rich global eclecticism: and doubtless such an ethical collage could be justified by the thought that different cultures are so many experiments in living and so should together supply the matter for a wise ethic. However, such an eclecticism would itself be in part consequence of some new worldview, and I would rather now persist with the question of what happens given our present range of worldviews, both religious and otherwise.

In line with my preliminary remarks I shall assume that there are some oppositions of religious imperatives (and secular imperatives), e.g. over abortion, marriage, the logic and nature of punishment, war, etc. as between different traditions and sub-traditions. Such oppositions are to be distinguished from alternatives. For instance, it is forbidden for orthopractic Jews to eat pork. A Christian has no such inhibition: but a situation in which the Christians and the Jew allow each other to practice their own way in this matter does not represent a contradiction. Alternatives can thus become a set of tolerated customary options. But behind such toleration there typically lurks a theory ('Such externals are not important', 'God laid this command on us but not on them', etc.)

As well as oppositions of imperatives there are differing emphases which might lead to divergent conduct, and these can arise both from basic attitudes and from differing models in history and myth. The theme of martyrdom is emphasized in Shi'i Islam but not in Theravada Buddhism; self-analysis is much more prominent in the latter than the former tradition, etc. These divergences in part derive from and in part are summed up in the differing focal figures such as Ali and Buddha.

The derivation of differing rules and emphases from the world-views is hardly strict: one can imagine a Catholicism without a ban on abortion and an Islam without martyrdom, even a Judaism without the ban on pork. But typically the ethical items get worked into an authoritative tradition – at its hardest a sacred scripture. It is here that the derivation can become subjectively certain. The item is seen by the believer as absolute and binding in so far as the canon has this quality (canon whether oral or written, etc.). Though notoriously the interpretations of authoritative traditions come to vary, nevertheless the insider – formed already by the variant interpretation – sees the preferred interpretation as authoritative, and often as quite certain (even if religion often goes with underlying doubts).

So a common, though not universal, aspect of worldviews is a 'hard' epistemology: an item is in the Canon, so it certainly must be binding: or it is the ruling of those in authority, so it certainly must be binding. The major question posed by the comparative study of religions (and worldview analysis) is how such oppositions of hard epistemologies can be resolved. For it inevitably turns out that crosscultural or crosstraditional arguments on behalf of my hard epistemology over yours are soft. Thus to argue for the Qur'an on the basis that it is wonderfully beautiful, resonant, awe-inspiring in its style – and how could an illiterate fellow have produced such a masterpiece? – is a soft argument depending first on esthetic judgments (wonderfully beautiful, etc.) and second on an alleged empirical impossibility (but who could have thought Mozart possible, before the event?). Actually, the arguments for hard epistemologies are doubly soft: they are soft in themselves, and they have to overcome the hurdles constituted by different worldviews, which not only are often institutionally entrenched, but also filter the arguments through different conceptual lenses. Concretely: if I am embedded in the Episcopal Church and see the world through Western Christian cosmopolitan eyes, the esthetic arguments about the Qur'an have a lot of inertial scepticism to overcome. And so we come to the following conclusive reasoning: the epistemology of a worldview is either hard or soft; but if it is hard it itself has to argue against conflicting epistemologies and the arguments it uses are bound to be soft; so the net result is that a worldview epistemology is soft. For soft arguments for the validity of a hard proof render the proof soft.

This is not a conclusion that is congenial to many religious or similar worldview believers. Their phenomenological certainty of faith collides with the outer judgment of uncertainty. This seems disagreeable and upsetting. The good news I suppose is that often we can be inwardly sure of things which we cannot prove or even persuade others about. We can contrast inner certitude and public certainty. They by no means go together. Even so, the conclusion is unsettling, for it licenses alternative and opposing views. It reflects the truth that the only proof in religion is internal to a system or tradition, and that is not enough. To put it another way, faith cannot produce external guarantees of its correctness. So how can it legitmately deny alternative ways and formulations of faith?

It will be replied that this is not how the situation is perceived in conservative seminaries and prestigious mosques, nor in sacred temples or totalitarian academies. I am not presenting these conclusions as a piece of phenomenology, but only as arising from the logic of the situation. We should note however that logic (in this loose sense) creates its own pressures. Those who resist the softness argument have to create more and more ingenious ways of keeping the situation concealed. The logic of the one world will have its slow effects, despite frontiers and visas of the mind.

But softness is not relativism: lack of proof in these matters does not imply that all positions are equal. For one thing a position which does not recognize epistemological softness is in that respect inferior to one which does. There are other tests of worldview – consonance with science, richness of relevant experience, capacity to bear fruits, etc. These are sometimes spiral (not circular but with an element of circularity) – e.g. the fruits: What if one faith produces persimmons and another oranges, because of a difference of value-emphasis?

The position I have sketched emphasizes the softness of epistemology, but does not go on to draw the conclusion of relativism, for there are soft reasons at least that can be deployed pro and contra differing worldviews. Soft non-relativism does not rob people of the quest for truth, but it does deprive them of the rights that pertain to being legitimately certain. There is no right therefore to teach your own worldview as though it alone could be true. Much, ethically and politically, flows from this.

First, it follows that we should be tolerant and understanding of the varied worldviews. Even if we are convinced of the absurdity of someone else's position we should remember that there are phases and forms of our own tradition or position which can likewise seem absurd, to ourselves or others or both.

Second, there is a Popperian argument from worldview-epistemology to politics as there is from science to politics. The open society which allows differing forms of belief and opinion is the best. At the level of doctrine, this pluralism is not hard to describe: the ways of allowing freedom of speech are well known. But what of customary oppositions? What about differing ethical and ritual practices? And what if a group decides it needs authoritarian arrangements internally in order to preserve its ethos and way of life?

As for customary oppositions, e.g. over abortions, then there is no question of stopping legitimate agitation and argument: obviously freedom of belief implies freedom of expression thereof. But this has something important to say about the question of authoritarian structures. It implies that if a group wants an authority figure it needs to set it up on a voluntary basis, for if people are free to criticise then only voluntarily can they suspend their freedom to criticize an authoritarian leader. That of course involves a seachange in many authoritarian groups: once they become voluntary the Leader in a strange way is elected.

But to be realistic: though we think of most such ethical and social questions as arising within a society – which for all practical purposes is a nation-State – a global ethic has to deal with a citizenship far beyond that milieu. Indeed, the soft non-relativist position is subversive of the nation-State in certain ways. I shall proceed to a discussion of the pressures of the argument in a moment. But let me first add a second main reason for us, in the context of comparative religious ethics, to espouse the open society. It is that opposition to knowledge about alternative world-views to the official one is the norm in worldview-closed societies (such as 18th-century Sweden or 20th-century East Germany). Often such studies are only possible in such monistic societies on condition that what is studied does not look like a live alternative option. Programmes in comparative religion tend to be exiguous in Marxist, Islamic and traditional Catholic countries; and in many other countries there is sometimes opposition from another direction – scientific–utilitarian humanism, as the dominant philosophy of the educated technocrat. The very attempt at a plural, descriptive comparative ethics is somewhat foreign to the totalitarian and authoritarian State. In any event, we are part, in this enterprise, of the open humanities and social sciences, whose flourishing presupposes a pluralistic politics.

Yet there is a paradox here. For – and this brings us back to the earlier discussion – our study concentrates on traditions of which Western liberalism is a major solvent, for it ends up with a disintegrative individualism. Are we then by our presuppositions, committed to the disappearance of what we study? There is no contradiction as such in this, but it is to say the least an eccentric pursuit to do this – though let it be remembered that the huntsman admires the fox, and the fisherperson the trout.

I slipped in the word 'Western' just above. Does the open and plural society need to be *Western*? There is nothing in my previous arguments to identify the open society with the West. On the contrary, it may be that in some respects other societies have a better understanding of pluralism than some typical Western democracies. For individualism as practised can, by majority pressure, paradoxically produce great conformism. The tendency of Western capitalism is to homogenize, so that gradually cultural differences are being eliminated. But be that as it may, the argument that openness is a precondition of our very subject adds an extra force to the argument from soft non-relativism. I now turn back to the question of a global as distinguished from a social, that is to say a national, ethic; and we can ask how non-relativism relates to this wider field.

It is perhaps wise to think of several factors relevant to the global milieu. When we use the world 'global' we are assuming that in some manner the life of humanity forms something of a system. That is now true. Especially since World War II this global system has become manifest. First, the period saw the rough completion of the process of distributing the land surface of the world among independent nation-States (and State-nations). Theoretically this international order is guaranteed by the United Nations Charter. In practice, it entrenches States' rights over against minorities' and individuals' rights, despite the Universal Declaration on Human Rights. Second, modern means of communication and transport have speeded up the process of the formation of a single global economic community – basically as capitalist order incorporating regions of socialism as part of the system, and dominated by a few hundred powerful multinational corporations. Third, travel and the media have created the framework for a world cultural superstructure, so that certain events like the Olympics have become phenomenologically world events. We are getting nearer de Chardin's noosphere as a unitary medium. At the moment it is embodied in an international set of overlapping elites: a kind of aristosphere. Fourth, there are a number of transnational agencies which help to bind the globe together or at least to mitigate the fragmentation represented by the system of nations. Among important transnationals are the aforementioned corporations; also there are intergovernment entities such as UNO, FAO and so on; there are global learned societies, consultative groups and the like; last but not least are the ecumenical religions, notably Christianity, Buddhism and Islam. In these, then, and other ways we can rightly think of ourselves as entering into a One World System; but an unstable one, not only because there can be crises in global capitalism, but more importantly because of the real possibility of the war to end wars.

In this global situation the role of the religions can be paradoxical. On the one hand the major faiths are transnational, and even those that are ethnically based (either because a religion is definitional of an ethnie or because it is an aspect of the ethnie's culture) can only persist on the tacit understanding that there is as it were a federal spirituality of which the ethnic religions are differing expressions. On the other hand the religions represent a problem of particularism, since they have in part rival views of right and wrong and of ultimate human happiness, etc., and these views affect social institutions. It seems to me that religious ethics are to be interpreted in the light of real possible global and troubles and disasters, such as the following:

> violent conflict between religions;
> war, including global war;
> widespread destruction of the natural environment;
> poverty and attendant evils, such as illiteracy, poor health, etc.;
> the oppression of minorities;
> the oppression of individuals;
> the painful destruction of traditions;
> widespread spiritual emptiness and lack of meaning.

There are other evils, of course, but these seem to be major ones. What does their treatment suggest about religious ethics?

First, even if we cannot attain unanimity on the contents of moral and political action, we can at least find in the moral strand overlapping beliefs in universal values. So a positive accentuation of these inter-religious overlaps conduces to a more unitary approach to human problems.

Second, soft non-relativism's drive towards toleration implies that it cannot be right to spread alternative views by force, save in so far as minimization of violence may itself be an issue (to which I come).

Third, as a corollary to the preceding, engagement in alternative modes of persuasion presupposes the validity of the proverb 'Never judge a man till you have walked a mile in his moccasins', i.e. the positive attempt to understand phenomenologically other people's viewpoints and values is always a correct endeavour.

Fourth, attention to the preceding three points implies that the rights of minorities within societies (i.e. nations) are something which the transnational and other religions ought to protect, within the limits of the minimization of violence.

Fifth, questions about the distribution of goods relate to the whole world, not just to the poor within a given society: so the religions need to promote a sense of universal sisterhood and citizenship in the kingdom of the dharma. In brief, religion is in principle internationalist, even when highly particularist. Likewise the environment is something held in trust for all citizens of the planet.

Sixth, in so far as the group of ultimate concern must be humanity (plus somewhat other living beings), and not the nation or ethnie or even the religious community of the elect, the rights of individuals become paramount – i.e. the right of a person simply because she is a member of the human race.

Seventh, the religions (and serious secular worldviews) should attempt to conserve or enhance meaning, partly by modernizing without violent ruptures, where possible, of the traditions which help to provide a framework of meaning, and partly by combating the trivialization of experience made possible with today's technological affluence.

Eighth, both because of soft non-relativism's implication of toleration and the use of means such as argument and example to spread one's ideas and values, and because of other considerations (compassion, etc.) the ecumenical and other religions ought to be or could agree at least on the principle of the minimization of violence. This is not to say that violence may never be justified: that depends in part with your worldview. But even the use of war should be conducted in the spirit of applying the least violence. This is a common, if oten hypocritically applied, defence of war.

Now to these remarks it may be replied that they are in part political imperatives. It is hard to separate politics from ethics; and it is obvious that many regimes would reject one or other of these theses I have been putting forward. But let me at least attempt to transpose these imperatives explicitly into personal terms, that is into the language of virtues rather than imperatives. What virtues do the theses imply? And how do they connect with traditional religious virtue? It seems to me that the virtues can be listed as follows:

generosity of spirit towards those holding other worldviews;
spiritual self-confidence;
the cultivation of imaginative empathy;
tenderness towards minorities;

the sense of universal brotherhood and justice;
reverence towards all as individuals;
the love of human meaning;
the attitude of non-violence.

Some of these are clearly covered by such traditional religious notions as that one should love one's neighbour/enemy; the *brahma-vihāras*; the Sufi notion of *jihad* as a spiritual struggle; the Islamic ideal of the brotherhood of humanity, etc.

It is of course clear that there are militant versions of religious and other worldviews which would only accept some of these putative virtues. Often wounded identity, a common collective condition in the modern age for various reasons, issues in vehemence of commitment; and 'realistic' politics suggests that one would become soft in the face of evil empires and the like were one to adopt these virtues. To this let me just add a few ripostes.

What makes an evil empire evil? Repression of minorities and individuals, the use of the propoganda of hate, threatening international behaviour. It is conceivable that in order to combat such it is necessary to use repression, hate and threats. But the justification for opposing evil then disappears. Even if some degree of threat of violence is needed to restrain violence, this would be justified as the minimization of violence which needs to be underpinned by attitudes of non-violence and universal brotherhood, etc. Moreover effective restraint of the other if violent requires an understanding of the other, and that implies imaginative empathy. So the virtues listed are not merely not inimicable to true *realpolitik* but are presupposed by it, if, that is, the *realpolitik* is on the side of the angels. If not, so what? We are after all discussing *ethics*, not self-interest.

However, there are thorny issues which these implications of soft non-relativism leave unresolved, and which I have skated round. They are issues concerned with not just freedom to express spiritual positions but to practice according to diverse systems of religious and other law. Should a Muslim in the United States be permitted to practice polygamy? Should Native Americans or the Amish have privileges in regard to the waiving of religion-State separation in the schools? Can pluralism in other words extend to intra-societal legal and ethical structures?

It may be noted that if the principles of individual and group freedom are applied – and these seem to be a consequence *inter alia* of soft non-relativism – customs can be practised privately on a voluntary basis: e.g. a widower and a widow can marry in Italy in Church but not register it as a civil wedding, which would lead to loss of certain pension rights. But the implication of our position is that pluralism does imply a voluntary basis for adherence to alternative and so different customary modes of living. There are moreover historical precedents which might if suitably adapted be made use of: the Ottoman millet system, the caste system (so far as it can be stated and implemented non-hierarchically), the cantonal system, etc. Even in the days of *cuius regio eius religio* there was usually freedom of migration if you did not wish to embrace your ruler's religion. It seems singularly inappropriate, other things being equal, that the majority's law should be forced upon a minority group (e.g. Islamic law being applied in the Christian and so-called 'animist' South Sudan). Even if some minority custom is offensive or repugnant to the majority there is room for discretion: and the majority in accordance with the virtues I have outlined might ask themselves whether their repugnance does not stem from a lack of imaginative empathy and of a sense of brotherhood, a lack of tenderness towards minorities, etc. Even if they be hard absolutists they may find echoes of these virtues in their traditional authoritative sources.

My total argument is from epistemology and global plurality. To rehearse its essence: some moral values are common and represent the primary thread in the moral strand. Others diverge because of differences of worldviews. Thus, since worldviews are not susceptible of proof and at best can only produce internal proofs of ethical rules, etc. the divergences between systems are not resolvable by proofs. The reasoning is soft, and the appropriate position to adopt is soft non-relativism. But this implies tolerant attitudes, which in world perspective imply certain religious attitudes, and certain virtues, notably those conducing to imaginative empathy, the minimization of violence and a sense of universal world citizenship.

Notes

CHAPTER 1 RELIGION AND THE WESTERN MIND

1. The best recent history is Eric J. Sharpe, *Comparative Religion – a History* (London: Duckworth, 1975); also very useful in Jacques Waardenburg (ed.), *Classical Approaches to the Study of Religion*, 2 vols (The Hague: Mouton, 1973–74).
2. *Schools Council Working Paper 36* (London: Methuen, 1971). See also Ninian Smart and Donald Horder (eds.), *New Movements in Religious Education* (London: Maurice Temple Smith, 1975).
3. I have discussed these points in *Worldviews: Crosscultural Explorations of Human Beliefs* (New York: Scribner's, 1983).

CHAPTER 2 THE POLITICAL IMPLICATIONS OF RELIGIOUS STUDIES

1. See Robert N. Bellah and Phillip Hammond, *Varieties of Civil Religion* (San Francisco: Harper & Row, 1980).
2. See David Martin, *A General Theory of Secularization* (Oxford: Blackwell, 1978).
3. *A Theory of Religious and Ideological Change: Illustrated from Modern South Asian and Other Religious Nationalisms* (Tempe: Department of Religious Studies, Arizona State University, 1984).
4. Willy Brandt, *Independent Commission on International Development Issues: Common Crisis North-South* (Cambridge, Mass.: MIT Press, 1983).
5. Karl Popper, *The Open Society and Its Enemies*, 5th edn rev. (Princeton University Press, 1966).

CHAPTER 3 THE INTELLECTUAL IMPLICATIONS OF RELIGIOUS STUDIES

1. As in: Richard Rorty, *Philosophy and the Mirror of Nature* (Princeton University Press, 1979); Thomas B. Kuhn, *The Structure of Scientific Revolutions* (Chicago University Press, 1963); Paul K. Feyerabend, *Against Method: an Outline of an Anarchistic Theory of Knowledge*

(Atlantic Highlands: Humanities Press, 1975); Hilary Putnam, *Realism and Reason* (Cambridge University Press, 1983).
2. Alasdair MacIntyre, *After Virtue* (London: Duckworth, 1981).
3. As in: Alvin Plantinga *God and Other Minds: a Study of the Rational Justification of Belief in God* (Ithaca, NY: Cornell University Press, 1967; Richard Swinburne, *The Existence of God* (Oxford University Press, 1978); and D. Z. Phillips, *The Concept of Prayer* (New York: Schocken, 1966).
4. As in: William A. Christian, Jr., *Person and God in a Spanish Valley* (New York: Seminar Press, 1972); Stanley J. Tambiah, *World Conqueror and World Renouncer* (Cambridge University Press, 1976) and *The Buddhist Saints of the Forest and the Cult of Amulets* (Cambridge University Press, 1984); and Richard Gombrich, *Precept and Practice* (Oxford: Clarendon Press, 1971).
5. See my Arizona university lecture in religion cited above, note 3, Chapter 2.
6. Peter Merkl and Ninian Smart (eds.), *Religion and Politics in the Modern World* (New York University Press, 1983).
7. Karl Barth, *Dogmatics in Outline*, translated by G. T. Thomson (New York: Philosophical Library, 1949); Hendrik Kraemer, *The Christian Message in a Non-Christian World* (The Edinburgh House Press, 1938).
8. Arnold Toynbee, *A Study of History*, abridged edn in one volume (Oxford University Press, 1972).

CHAPTER 5   RESURGENCE AND IDENTITY IN THREE
FAITHS

1. See my recent *Worldviews: Crosscultural Explorations of Human Beliefs* (New York: Scribner's, 1983).
2. See 'Religion, Myth and Nationalism', *Scottish Journal of Religious Studies*, vol. 1, no. 1.
3. A good treatment of all this is Richard Quebedeaux, *By Whose Authority* (San Francisco: Harper & Row, 1981) esp. p. 169 and 138ff.
4. See Charles Wendell (ed.) *Five Tracts of Hasan Al-Bannā (1906–49)* (Berkeley: University of California Press, 1978).
5. Hence the preoccupations of many modern Muslim historiographers: see Yvonne Yazbeck Haddad, *Contemporary Islam and the Challenge of History* (Albany: SUNY Press, 1982) esp. p. 83ff.
6. As an example Fred R. von der Mehden, in John L. Esposito, (ed.), *Islam and Development: Relgion and Sociopolitical Change* (Syracuse University Press, 1980) esp. p. 169. See also in the same volume the perceptive essary by John Alden Williams, 'Veiling in Egypt as a Political and Social Phenomenon', pp. 71–86.
7. In an earlier generation Billy Sunday had said 'Christianity and patriotism are synonymous' (Quebedeaux, op. cit., p. 28).
8. Gil Carl Alroy, *Attitudes Towards Jewish Statehood in the Arab World* (New York: American Association for Peace in the Middle East, 1971)

pp. 1–69; and Rael Jean Isaac *Israel Divided: Ideological Politics in the Jewish State* (Baltimore: The Johns Hopkins University Press, 1976) p. 158.
9. Isaac, op. cit., p. 138ff.
10. E. Rosenthal *Islam in the Moslem National State* (Cambridge University Press, 1965) pp. 291ff.
11. Esposito in Esposito, op. cit., ch. 8.
12. See David Holden and Richard Johns, *The House of Saud* (London: Pan Books, 1981) ch. 25 (written by James Buchan).

Bibliography

Alroy, Gil Carl, *Attitudes Towards Jewish Statehood in the Arab World* (New York: American Association for Peace in the Middle East, 1971).

Barth, Karl, *Dogmatics in Outline*, tr, G. T. Thomson (New York: Philosophical Library, 1949).

Bellah, Robert N. and Hammond, Phillip, *Varieties of Civil Religion* (San Francisco: Harper & Row, 1980).

Brandt, Willy, *Independent Commission on International Development Issues: Common Crisis North-South* (Cambridge, Mass.: MIT Press, 1983).

Christian, William A., Jr. *Person and God in a Spanish Valley* (NY Seminar Press, 1972).

Esposito, John, *Islam and Development: Religion and Scociopolitical Change* (Syracuse University Press, 1980).

Feyerabend, Paul K., *Against Method: an Anarchistic Theory of Knowledge* (Atlantic Highlands, NJ: Humanities Press, 1983).

Gombrich, Richard, *Precept and Practice* (Oxford: Clarendon Press, 1971).

Haddad, Yvonne Yazbeck, *Contemporary Islam and the Challenge of History* (Albany: SUNY Press, 1982).

Holden, David and Johns, Richard, with James Buchan, *The House of Saud* (London: Pan Books, 1981).

Horder, Donald and Smart, Ninian (eds.) *New Movements in Religious Education* (London: Maurice Temple Smith, 1975).

Isaac, Rael Jean, *Israel Divided: Ideological Politics in the Jewish State* (Baltimore: The Johns Hopkins University Press, 1976).

Kraemer, Hendrik, *The Christian Message in a Non-Christian World* (Edinburgh House Press, 1938).

Kuhn, Thomas, *The Structure of Scientific Revolutions* (Chicago University Press, 1975).

MacIntyre, Alasdair, *After Virtue* (London: Duckworth, 1981).

Martin, David, *A General Theory of Secularization* (New York: Harper & Row, 1978).

Merkl, Peter and Smart, Ninian (eds.), *Religion and Politics in the Modern World* (New York University Press, 1983).

Phillips, D. Z., *The Concept of Prayer* (New York, Schocken, 1966).

Plantinga, Alvin, *God and Other Minds* (Ithaca, NY: Cornell University Press, 1967).

Popper, Karl, *The Open Society and Its Enemies*, 5th ed rev. (Princeton University Press, 1966).

Putnam, Hilary, *Realism and Reason* (Cambridge University Press, 1983).

Quebedeaux, Richard, *By Whose Authority* (San Francisco: Harper & Row, 1981).

Rorty, Richard, *Philosophy and the Mirror of Nature* (Princeton University Press, 1979).

Rosenthal, E., *Islam in the Modern National State* (Cambridge University Press, 1965).

Sharpe, Eric, J., *Comparative Religion – a History* (London: Duckworth, 1975).

Smart, Ninian, *Concept and Empathy* (London: Macmillan, 1986).

　Beyond Ideology (London: Collins, 1981).

　Worldviews (New York: Scribner's, 1983).

　The Science of Religion and the Sociology of Knowledge (Princeton University Press, 1973).

Swinburne, Richard, *The Existence of God* (Oxford University Press, 1978).

Tambiah, Stanley, *The Buddhist Saints of the Forest and the Cult of Amulets* (Cambridge University Press, 1984).

Toynbee, Arnold, *A Study of History*, abridged edn (Oxford University Press, 1972).

Waardenburg, Jacques, *Classical Approaches to the Study of Religion*, 2 vols (The Hague: Mouton, 1973–74).

Wallerstein, Immanuel, *The Modern World-System* (NY: Academic Press, 1976).

Wendell, Charles, *Five Tracts of Hasan Al-Bannā* (Berkeley: University of California Press, 1978).

Index